AMERICAN POETS PROJECT

THE NEGLECTED MASTERS AWARD

WAS ESTABLISHED BY

The Poetry Foundation

*and this volume is published in conjunction
with that honor*

————

AMERICAN POETS PROJECT

is published with a gift in memory of

James Merrill

and support from its Founding Patrons

Sidney J. Weinberg, Jr. Foundation

The Berkley Foundation

Richard B. Fisher & Jeanne Donovan Fisher

Anne Stevenson

selected poems

andrew motion editor

AMERICAN POETS PROJECT

THE LIBRARY OF AMERICA

Introduction, volume compilation, and notes copyright © 2008 by Literary Classics of the United States, Inc. All rights reserved. Printed in the United States of America. No part of this book may be reproduced in any manner whatsoever without permission.

The poems in this volume appeared in slightly different form in *The Collected Poems 1955–1995*, *Poems 1955–2005*, and *Stone Milk* copyright © 2000, 2005, 2007 by Anne Stevenson. Reproduced by permission of Bloodaxe Books. Copyright © 2008 by Anne Stevenson.

The paper used in this publication meets the minimum requirements of the American National Standard for Information Sciences—Permanence of Paper for Printed Library Materials, ANSI Z39.48—1984.

Design by Chip Kidd and Mark Melnick.
Frontispiece: Annie Lennox

Library of Congress Control Number: 2007941727
ISBN 978-1-59853-019-3
American Poets Project—26

10 9 8 7 6 5 4 3 2 1

Anne
Stevenson

CONTENTS

Introduction   **xiii**

Selected Shorter Poems

Living in America   **3**

The Garden of Intellect   **4**

Still Life in Utah   **5**

Ann Arbor   **5**

Sierra Nevada   **7**

The Spirit Is Too Blunt an Instrument   **9**

Poem for a Daughter   **10**

The Mother   **11**

Siskin   **12**

Generations   **12**

Coming Back to Cambridge   **13**

North Sea off Carnoustie   **15**

By the Boat House, Oxford   **17**

Ragwort   **17**

The Minister   **18**

Enough of Green   **19**

Path   **20**

Between   **20**

The Circle   **21**

The Sun Appears in November   22

Meniscus   22

The Price   23

If I Could Paint Essences   24

Small Philosophical Poem   25

Ah Babel   26

Swifts   27

Himalayan Balsam   29

The Fish Are All Sick   31

In the Tunnel of Summers   32

Waving to Elizabeth   33

After the Fall   34

Two Poems for Frances Horovitz

    Red Rock Fault   35

    Willow Song   36

Dreaming of the Dead   38

The Fiction Makers   39

Making Poetry   42

A Dream of Stones   43

Trinity at Low Tide   44

Salter's Gate   45

Cold   47

Washing the Clocks   48

Politesse   49

Bloody Bloody   51

Black Hole   53

Lost   54

Journal Entry: Impromptu in C Minor   55

Letter to Sylvia Plath   59

The Other House   63

Elegy   65

When the camel is dust it goes through the needle's eye   68

Where the Animals Go   69

As I Lay Sleeping   70

Saying the World   71
Vertigo   72
A Surprise on the First Day of School   72
Arioso Dolente   73
Moonrise   75
Skills   76
An Angel   77
Granny Scarecrow   79
Leaving   80
On Going Deaf   81
To witness pain is a different form of pain   82
Postscriptum   83
A Report from the Border   84
Haunted   84
Hearing with My Fingers   85
A Marriage   86
Washing My Hair   87
Who's Joking with the Photographer?   88
To Phoebe   90
In the Weather of Deciduous Souls   90
Stone Milk   91
Before Eden   92
The Enigma   95
Orcop   96
Inheriting My Grandmother's Nightmare   97
Beach Kites   99
Variations on a Line by Peter Redgrove   100

Correspondences: A Family History in Letters   103

Biographical Note   199
Index   201

INTRODUCTION

Anne Stevenson is one of the most remarkable poetic voices to have emerged on either side of the Atlantic in the last fifty years. Her work covers an impressively wide range—from large-scale narratives to finely wrought lyrics—and is cleverly tuned to history but full of edgy individuality. In certain respects her achievement has been properly recognized: she has won several important prizes and generally found critical approval. Yet because she has never found the large general readership that she deserves, she can also be called a "neglected writer." Although the phrase has an inevitably melancholy ring to it, in Stevenson's case it is also proof of quality. She has always spurned the siren songs of mere fashionability; she has deliberately placed herself at the edge of orthodoxies; and she has made a virtue of remaining restless in her travels and placements as well as her thinking. This means the present *Selected Poems* has to embrace a paradox. It must aspire to win her a larger audience while at the same time honouring the qualities that prove her independence. It must show the ways in which her poetry utters general truths in an approachable idiom, but also celebrate its very particular insights and articulations.

In the biographical note to her collection *Granny Scarecrow*, published in 2000 when she was sixty-seven, we are told that Stevenson was "born in England of American parents, grew up in the States, but has lived in Britain for most of her adult life." This is fair enough, but as a resumé it can only hint at the questions that dominate her work. How does a personality define itself within a family? How does child-love translate into loving as an adult? What role do places play in the creation of a sensibility? And in particular: What is the relationship between thinking about questions of belonging, and observing the hard facts of location and habitat? At a time when political and social upheavals around the world have provoked many poets to consider the enigmas of arrival, Stevenson has produced a large body of work that is at once representative of common contemporary concerns and generously personal. She is a voice for our age and compellingly her own questing and questioning self.

Stevenson's originality is of a complex and multi-layered kind. As a student at the University of Michigan she began to write poetry while studying the challenges to puritanism in American writers such as Robert Frost and Elizabeth Bishop, of whom she later wrote a pioneering study. In the late 1980s she developed many related ideas in her biography of Sylvia Plath. (When it first appeared, this book was considered controversial in its even-handed treatment of Plath's marriage to Ted Hughes; other subsequent studies of the relationship have done a good deal to justify the approach.) Instead of trying to conceal the influence of these writers in her work, Stevenson openly addresses them in a number of poems, deliberately echoes them, and consciously allies herself to many of their practices. The effect is not in the least to compromise her authenticity; rather, it establishes the foundations of her work in a distinct tradition. She is herself a puritan writer who at once honors and contests her inheritance; writing in the heat generated by this personal conflict, she has forged a style that both registers and stands apart from the confessional modes and political dogmas of later twentieth-century women's poetry.

Stevenson's longest and best-sustained poetic examination of the puritan past is *Correspondences* (1974), the poem-cycle that first established her reputation in England following her departure from America and that provides a broad background to the rest of her writing. Its piecemeal family history—in which much of the material for the puritan Boyds is modelled on her mother's family, while her father's is represented by the more worldly Arbeiters—comprises letters, lyrics, and prose poems. It is at once a collection of wistfully entertained backward glances and a proof that Stevenson accepts the inevitability of change and challenge. In this respect, *Correspondences* anticipates her other and later long poem *A Lament for the Makers* (published in 2007 but not included here for reasons of space), in which she converses with the poets who have meant most to her across the years. *Correspondences* presents a drama of identity in a domestic context, *A Lament* does the same thing in literary terms. For both poems, the issue is not how to escape the past, but how to accommodate the past in the present; how to preserve its values and authenticities without becoming trapped in nostalgia or sapped by historical example.

The same questions are present from the outset in Stevenson's shorter pieces. We find them in one of the earliest lyrics in her first *Collected Poems* (1996), "To My Daughter in a Red Coat," where she says:

Child, your mittens tug your sleeves.
They lick your drumming feet, the leaves.
You come so fast, so fast.

You violate the past,
My daughter, as your coat dances.

They emerge again in many of her narrative poems—"The Dear Ladies of Cincinnati," for instance, in which we meet "the aunts" who "remembered the words of hit tunes they'd been courted to,/avoided the contagion of thought/ so successfully that the game kept time to the music." And they circle too in the majority of her later poems about family matters. "Of course I love them," she says of her children in "The Mother." "That is my daughter and this is my son./And this is my life I give them to please them./It has never been used. Keep it safe, pass it on."

For all their general resonance, many of these shorter family poems arise from the same particular circumstances that Stevenson remembers in *Correspondences*. She was brought up in the university environments of Harvard, Yale, and Ann Arbor by parents she has called "intelligent and sympathetic." From her father, the philosopher C. L. Stevenson, she absorbed a love of classical music and an intolerance of unexamined, conformist opinion—as we discover in "Elegy," where music (and by implication all the arts, including poetry) is described as a means of re-interpreting the past, and where philosophy is by implication commended as a way of challenging accepted truths. It was her mother, however, who instilled in her a love of history together with the sturdy compassion that lies at the root of her poetry. We can see this in "Arioso Dolente," for instance, where Stevenson refers to her mother as someone "who read and thought and poured herself into me;/ she was the jug and I was the two-eared cup./How she would scorn today's 'show-biz inanity,/democracy twisted, its high ideals sold up!'"

Although Stevenson clearly owes debts to the traditions represented by her parents, these have done as much to provoke her sense of detachment as they have to stimulate a sense of belonging. For one thing, her father's work as a university teacher apparently bred in her a love-hate relationship with academies, which often produces sideswipes at their apparent desiccation and fustiness. In "Ann Arbor" we hear about "the usual/academic antipathies"; in "Coming Back to Cambridge" we find dons and their wives who are "Arrogant./Within the compass of wistfulness"; and in "By the Boat House, Oxford" we meet more academic wives "in their own quenched country" who are half-pitied and half-scorned for believing their husbands are "plainly superior." For another, Stevenson's father, in particular, set her a vital example about the value of intellectual restlessness—restlessness that formed a part of her compulsion to move from America to England, and then to spend much of her adult life moving around and laying claim to different parts of her adopted country: Cambridge, Oxford, the Welsh borders, Wales itself, the North-East.

The question Stevenson wants to answer in many of her early poems is not "when will I arrive at the one stable place I might call home," but "how can I benefit from and understand what it means to keep moving." In the work of her early maturity, it seems that sexual and married love might help her reach a conclusion. Yet for all their force and candor, her love poems habitually describe human tenderness in terms of landscape—suggesting that for her "home" will finally involve places more reliably than people. In the brief and potent lyric "New York," she wonders if "love, love, love/is the only green in the jungle"; in "Reversals", she asks ". . . is love in its last metamorphosis arable,/less than what was sometimes imaginary,/more than what was usually accessible—/full furrows harvested, a completed sky?"

This shift of trust away from individuals to their

surroundings is often accompanied by forthright doubting of herself and others. "There only is one love—/which is never enough" we hear in "Theme with Variations," and in "The Marriage" she says with wry deprecation:

> Even as it is,
> there are compensations
> for having to meet
> nose to neck
> chest to scapula
> groin to rump
> when they sleep.
> They look, at least,
> as if they were going
> in the same direction.

(Strikingly, the personal difficulties registered here are often connected to the complications of raising children—complications that are linked to the family—matters raised more generally elsewhere. "A woman's life is her own/until it is taken away/by a first particular cry," she says in "Poem for a Daughter.")

Throughout Stevenson's fully mature work, this question of how to continue living in transit, and yet have an adequate sense of belonging, becomes her dominant theme. The title of her first selected poems, *Travelling Behind Glass* (1974), suggestively indicates that a part of her restlessness derives from the sense that she is falsely protected from reality. (As she says in "The Price": "My dear, the ropes that bind us/are safe to hold;/the walls that crush us/keep us from the cold.") It is therefore not surprising that she should be strongly drawn to landscapes that are themselves fluid, or marginal—to borders and border-counties, to water and shorelines ("The sea is as near as we come to another world," she writes in "North Sea off Carnoustie"), and to objects that are either a kind of boundary in themselves (glass, for instance) or a reminder of mobility. In the same way her large number of good poems about birds, for example, tend to celebrate migratory species (such as swifts); and her similarly strong poems about flora and fauna often dwell on ideas of escape or transgression. "Ragwort" is characteristic:

> They won't let railways alone, these ragged flowers.
> They're some remorseless joy of dereliction
> Darkest banks exhale like vivid breath
> as bricks divide to let them root between.
> How every falling place concocts their smile,
> taking what's left and making a song of it.

There is another and even larger reason for Stevenson to insist on the need to keep moving, keep enquiring. This has less to do with her sense of being adrift in the physical world than of being philosophically in two minds. In much the same sense that she feels she is living between generations, between certain kinds of landscape, between certain named places and certain loved individuals, so she also feels divided between different kinds of response to experience. Early in her writing life, there are signs that Stevenson feels tempted to heal this division by abolishing herself. In the poem "Travelling Behind Glass," for instance, we hear her ask for

> . . . a sea
> to be accommodating,
> to warm me, obey me,
> accept me like an arm;
> in time to release me
> entirely, as nothing at all.
> As belonging to nothing at all.

As her work develops, she finds a bolder and more subtle solution to her dilemma—one that involves her in making repeated efforts to distinguish between a thought-filled response to the world, and one which depends on more sensuous kinds of appreciation and involvement.

We can see the differences being weighed in the aptly titled "Small Philosophical Poem," which sets "the pleasure of thought" experienced by Dr Animus against the more material existence of his wife, Anima. Short as it is, this lyric establishes the integrity as well as the aridity of the doctor's position, and the warmth (the "love") as well as the vulnerability (the "fear") of his wife's—implying at its close that although Anima must bear the burdens of her consciousness, they nevertheless connect her with the world in more valuable ways than any her husband has at his disposal. A similar point is made in the elegy for Anne Pennington, "Dreaming of the Dead," where Stevenson says

> Oh, I am what I see and know,
> But no other solid thing's there
>
> Except for the terrible glow
> Of your face and its quiet belief,
> Light wood ash falling like snow
>
> On my weaker grief.

Such poems form the bedrock of Stevenson's work because they prove that her final commitment as a writer is to the ragged, volatile, and familiarly uncertain world, not to a version of experience that has been tidied up to fit a controlling idea. But it is also a mark of her quality as a poet, and further proof of her need for continual self-testing, that this commitment is never entirely fixed and settled. The surfaces of her best work, which are always impressively alive to the significance of things-in-themselves, are repeatedly disturbed by incursions from the thinking mind. These make her in the best sense an uncomfortable writer—one whose inheritance (which promoted notions of honesty, austerity, and philosophical rigor) has led to her cautious acceptance that art can look faithfully at the evolutionary fleetingness of human life without paying lip service to a righteous God or a benevolent-minded Designer. As she has said herself, "If my poems have any value as art, it is because they ARE art. What I really learned from Elizabeth Bishop (and from Sylvia Plath too) is that poetry matters when content, form, passion unite in language that speaks to the ear and heart as much as to the mind—to body and soul, you might say, as a single, always threatened, always perishable entity."

It's not just that Stevenson refuses to settle for easy conclusions about what makes a personality complete, and about what makes life bearable; she is also and often agitated by the act of writing itself —debating how it can best shoulder its responsibilities, and manifest the contradictory truths of nature. In the majority of her poems, these agitations are given a local habitation and a name: they arise in particular relationships and particular landscapes. They also stand clear in a handful of poems about writing itself. Some of these question the ability of language to capture what it seeks to express—"the inescapable ache/of trying to catch, say, the catness of cat/as he crouches, stalking his shadow,/on the other side of the window." Others (and especially in her book *The Fiction Makers*, 1985), call the entire business of writing into question: "In the event/the event is sacrificed/to a fiction of its having happened." Others again, and particularly those that mention her increasing deafness, go so far as to wonder whether her faith in seeking to comprehend the world through the senses is in fact well-founded. But while these questions are posed in all seriousness (or seriously laughing) they are never allowed to undermine her faith in first principles. The devastations of philosophy always prove weaker than the consolations of mystery, form, and sympathetic wit—as we can see in her typically courageous short poem "On Going Deaf":

> I've lost a sense. Why should I care?
> Searching myself, I find a spare.
> I keep that sixth sense in repair
> And set it deftly, like a snare.

A part of what Stevenson means by "that sixth sense" is the imagination itself, and it is right and proper than any introduction to her work should end by insisting on its authority in her work. She is not much given to plundering her unconscious (however interested she might be in dream-stories), and neither does she often yeast up her language to evoke surreal states of mind. But she does continually animate her acts of clear-seeing by connecting the exterior world with her interior states. It is, of course, a connection that all poets make to a greater or lesser extent, but in her case the fusions have a particular resonance. They are the means by which Stevenson stays true to her inheritance even as she extends it. They are proof that she is a puritan writer who is both at peace and at odds with herself. Her work is continually fortified by that contradiction, for reasons that she makes plain—appropriately enough—at the end of her kindred-spirit "Letter to Sylvia Plath":

> We learn to be human when we kneel
> To imagination, which is real
> long after reality is dead
> and history has put its bones to bed.

Andrew Motion
2007

SELECTED SHORTER POEMS

Living in America

'Living in America,'
the intelligent people at Harvard say,
'is the price you pay for living in New England.'

Californians think
living in America is a reward
for managing not to live anywhere else.

The rest of the country?
Could it be sagging between two poles,
tastelessly decorated, dangerously overweight?

No. Look closely.
Under cover of light and noise
both shores are hurrying towards each other.

San Francisco
is already half way to Omaha.
Boston is nervously losing its way in Detroit.

Desperately the inhabitants
hope to be saved in the middle.
Pray to the mountains and deserts to keep them apart.

The Garden of Intellect

It's too big to begin with.
There are too many windless gardens
Walled to protect eccentric vegetation
From a crude climate.
Rare shoots, reared in glass until
Old enough to reproduce themselves,
Wholly preoccupy the gardeners
Who deliberately find it difficult
To watch each other, having planted themselves
Head downward with their glasses
In danger of falling off over their thumbs.

Some beds bear nearly a thousand petunias;
Others labour to produce one rose.
Making sense of the landscape, marking distinctions,
Neat paths criss-cross politely,
Shaping mauve, indigo and orange hexagons,
Composing triangles and circles
To make the terrain seem beautiful.

But to most of the inhabitants
These calculated arrangements are
Not only beautiful but necessary.
What they cultivate protects, is protected from
The man-eating weeds of the wilderness,
Roses of imaginary deserts,
Watered by mirage, embellished
By brilliant illusory foliage, more real
For having neither name nor substance.

Still Life in Utah

Somewhere nowhere in Utah, a boy by the roadside,
gun in his hand, and the rare dumb hard tears flowing.
Beside him, the greyheaded man has let one arm slide
awkwardly over his shoulders, is talking and pointing
at whatever it is, dead, in the dust on the ground.

By the old parked Chevy, two women, talking and
    watching.
Their skirts flag forward, bandannas twist with their
    hair.
Around them, sheep and a fence and the sagebrush
    burning
and burning with a blue flame. In the distance, where
mountains are clouds, lightning, but no rain.

Ann Arbor

(A Profile)

Neither city nor town, its location,
even, is ambiguous.
Of North and East and Middlewest it is
and is not; in every sense,
a hopeless candidate for the picturesque.
Trees and a few grand accidentally preserved
eyesores save it from total suburbanisation,
give it the mildly authentic complexion
of secondhand furniture.

No setting for tragedy,
it is the scene, nonetheless, for more
than its surfeit of traffic would suggest.
Entrances and exits are frequent enough
to be anonymous as each year the young
adolesce in its residences, the usual
academic antipathies liven the cocktail parties.
Hard done by, driven from their garrets,
thin graduate students gripe in the beer joints,
leaving their wives to cope with babies
and contemporary interior decoration.

In all the tongues of the world
its tone is Germanic and provincial.
Yugoslavs, Hindus, Japanese
fraternise in the supermarkets
where beansprouts and braunschweiger
are equally available.
Love is frequently experienced over
jugs of California claret, politics are important,
and culture so cheap and convenient
that every evening you expect thin strains of Mozart
to issue from half a dozen windows.

The women who do not run for alderman
paint pictures, write poetry or give expensive parties
for the members of visiting symphony orchestras.
Their children are well-fed, rude and intelligent,
while, alone in immense mysterious houses, witches
remember the coaches of the first city fathers.

A microcosm, a mosaic, always paradoxical,
with scenery it has little to do.
And if you venerate antiquity or feel wiser
where there is history, you will, of course,
prefer Cambridge, though even there
the proportion of good people to bad architecture
is probably about the same.

(1961)

Sierra Nevada

(*for Margaret Elvin, 1963*)

Landscape without regrets whose weakest junipers
    strangle and split granite,
whose hard, clean light is utterly without restraint,
    whose mountains can purify and dazzle
and every minute excite us, but never can offer us
    commiseration, never can tell us
anything about ourselves except that we are
    dispensable . . .

The rocks and water. The glimmering rocks, the
          hundreds and hundreds of blue lakes
ought to be mythical, while the great trees, soon as they
          die, immediately become ghosts,
stalk upright among the living with awful composure.
          But even these bones that light
has taken and twisted, with their weird gesticulations
          and shadows that look as if
they'd been carved out of dust, even these
have nothing to do with what we have done or not done.

Now, as we climb on the high bare slopes,
          the most difficult earth
supports the most delicate flowers: gilia and harebells,
          kalmia and larkspur, everywhere
wild lupin's tight blue spires and fine-fingered
          handshaped leaves.
Daintiest of all, the low mariposa, lily of the mountain,
with its honey stained cup and no imperfect dimension.

If we stand in the fierce but perfectly transparent wind
          we can look down over the boulders,
over the drifted scree with its tattered collar of
          manzanita,
          over the groves of hemlock,
the tip of each tree resembling an arm
          extended to a drooping forefinger,
down, down, over the whole, dry, difficult
          train of the ascent, down to the lake
with its narrow, swarming edges where little white boats
          are moving their oars like waterbugs.

Nothing but the wind makes noise.
The lake, transparent to its greeny brown floor,
        is everywhere else bluer than the sky.
The boats hardly seem to touch its surface. Just as
        this granite cannot really touch us,
although we stand here and name the colours of its
        flowers.

The wind is strong without knowing that it is wind.
        The twisted tree that is not warning
or supplicating, never considers that it is not wind.
        We think
if we were to stay here for a long time, lie here
        like wood on these waterless beaches,
we would forget our names, would remember that
        what we first wanted
had something to do with stones, the sun,
the thousand colours of water, brilliances, blues.

The Spirit Is Too Blunt an Instrument

The spirit is too blunt an instrument
to have made this baby.
Nothing so unskilful as human passions
could have managed the intricate
exacting particulars: the tiny
blind bones with their manipulating tendons,
the knee and the knucklebones, the resilient
fine meshings of ganglia and vertebrae,
the chain of the difficult spine.

Observe the distinct eyelashes and sharp crescent
fingernails, the shell-like complexity
of the ear, with its firm involutions
concentric in miniature to minute
ossicles. Imagine the
infinitesimal capillaries, the flawless connections
of the lungs, the invisible neural filaments
through which the completed body
already answers to the brain.

Then name any passion or sentiment
possessed of the simplest accuracy.
No, no desire or affection could have done
with practice what habit
has done perfectly, indifferently,
through the body's ignorant precision.
It is left to the vagaries of the mind to invent
love and despair and anxiety
and their pain.

Poem for a Daughter

'I think I'm going to have it,'
I said, joking between pains.
The midwife rolled competent
sleeves over corpulent milky arms.
'Dear, you never have it,
we deliver it.'
A judgement years proved true.
Certainly I've never had you

as you still have me, Caroline.
Why does a mother need a daughter?
Heart's needle, hostage to fortune,
freedom's end. Yet nothing's more perfect
than that bleating, razor-shaped cry
that delivers a mother to her baby.
The bloodcord snaps that held
their sphere together. The child,
tiny and alone, creates the mother.

A woman's life is her own
until it is taken away
by a first particular cry.
Then she is not alone
but part of the premises
of everything there is:
a time, a tribe, a war.
When we belong to the world
we become what we are.

The Mother

Of course I love them, they are my children.
That is my daughter and this my son.
And this is my life I give them to please them.
It has never been used. Keep it safe, pass it on.

Siskin

(Glasgow, 1967)

Small bird with green plumage,
yellow to green to white
on the underparts, yes, a siskin
alive on my own cedar,
winter visitor, resident in Scotland,
wholly himself.

I saw him, and you, too,
alive again,
thin but expert, seated
with your bird-glasses, bird book
and concentrated expression,
hoping for siskins in Vermont.

He pleased me for your sake—
not so much as he would have pleased you.
Unless it was you he came for,
and I something you inhabited
from the second his green flame
flickered in that black tree
to the next second when he was gone.

Generations

Know this mother by her three smiles:
A grey one drawn over her mouth by frail hooks,
A hurt smile under each eye.

Know this mother by the frames she makes.
By the silence in which she suffers each child
To scratch out the aquatints in her mind.

Know this mother by the way she says
'Darling' with her teeth clenched,
By the fabulous lies she cooks.

Coming Back to Cambridge

(*England, 1971*)

Casual, almost unnoticeable,
it happens every time you return.
Somewhere along the flat road in
you lose to voluptuous levels
between signposts to unnecessary dozing villages
every ghost of yourself but Cambridge.
Somewhere—by Fen Drayton or Dry Drayton,
by the finger pointing aimlessly to Over—
you slip into a skin that lives
perpetually in Cambridge.

It knows where you are.

As you drive you watch a workman
wheel a bicycle around a stile,
hump onto the saddle and
ride off past a field of cows.
A few stop chewing to stare.

And you know where you are even before
the landmarks (beautiful to the excluded)
begin to accumulate.
The stump of the Library.
The lupin spire of the Catholic Church.
Four spikey blossoms on King's.
The Round Church, a mushroom in this
forest of Gothic and traffic and
roses too perfect to look alive.

The river is the same—conceited,
historic, full of the young.
The streets are the same. And around them
the same figures, the same cast with a
change of actors, move as if concentric
to a radiance without location.
The pupils of their eyes glide sideways,
apprehensive of martyrdom to which
they might not be central.
They can never be sure.
Great elations could be happening without them.

And just as the hurrying, preoccupied dons
tread the elevations of their detachment and yet
preserve an air of needing to be protected,
so, also, these wives choosing vegetables in the market,
these schoolchildren in squadrons,
these continental girl-friends and black men,
these beards, these bicycles, these
skinny boys fishing, these lovers of the pubs,
these lovers of the choirboys, these intense shrill

ladies and gaunt, fanatical burnt out old women
are all more than this. Arrogant.
Within the compass of wistfulness.

Nothing that really matters really exists.

But the statues are alive.
You can walk in and out of the picture.
Though the mild façades harden before and
behind you like stereographs, within them
there is much to be taken for granted.
Meals and quarrels, passions and inequalities.
A city like any other, were it not for the
order at the centre and the high
invisible bridge it is built upon,
with its immense views of an intelligible human
        landscape
into which you never look without longing to enter;
into which you never fall without the curious struggle
        back.

North Sea off Carnoustie

You know it by the northern look of the shore,
by salt-worried faces,
an absence of trees, an abundance of lighthouses.
It's a serious ocean.

Along marram-scarred, sandbitten margins
wired roofs straggle out to where
a cold little holiday fair
has floated in and pitched itself
safely near the prairie of a golf course.
Coloured lights have sunk deep into the solid wind,
but all they've caught is a pair of lovers
and three silly boys.
Everyone else has a dog.
Or a room to get to.

The smells are of fish and of sewage and cut grass.
Oystercatchers, doubtful of habitation,
clamour *weep, weep, weep*, as they fuss over
scummy black rocks the tide leaves for them.

The sea is as near as we come to another world.

But there in your stony and windswept garden
a blackbird is confirming the grip of the land.
You, you, he murmurs, dark purple in his voice.

And now in far quarters of the horizon
lighthouses are awake, sending messages—
invitations to the landlocked,
warnings to the experienced,
but to anyone returning from the planet ocean,
candles in the windows of a safe earth.

By the Boat House, Oxford

They belong here in their own quenched country.
I had forgotten nice women could be so nice,
smiling beside large sons on the makeshift quay,
frail, behind pale faces and hurt eyes.

Their husbands are plainly superior, with them, without
    them.
Their boys wear privilege like a clean inheritance, easily.
(Now a swan's neck couples with its own reflection,
making in the simple water a perfect 3.)

The punts seem resigned to an unexciting mooring.
But the women? It's hard to tell. Do their fine grey hairs
and filament lips approve or disdain the loving
that living alone, or else lonely in pairs, impairs?

Ragwort

They won't let railways alone, these ragged flowers.
They're some remorseless joy of dereliction
Darkest banks exhale like vivid breath
as bricks divide to let them root between.
How every falling place concocts their smile,
taking what's left and making a song of it.

The Minister

We're going to need the minister
to help this heavy body into the ground.

But he won't dig the hole;
others who are stronger and weaker will have to do that.
And he won't wipe his nose and his eyes;
others who are weaker and stronger will have to do that.
And he won't bake cakes or take care of the kids—
women's work. Anyway,
what would they do at a time like this
if they didn't do that?

No, we'll get the minister to come
and take care of the words.

He doesn't have to make them up,
he doesn't have to say them well,
he doesn't have to like them
so long as they agree to obey him.

We have to have the minister
so the words will know where to go.

Imagine them circling and circling
the confusing cemetery.
Imagine them roving the earth
without anywhere to rest.

Enough of Green

Enough of green,
though to remember childhood
is to stand in uneasy radiance
under those trees.

Enough yellow.
We are looking back
over our shoulders, telling our children
to be happy.

Try to forget about red.
Leave it to the professionals.
But perceive heaven as a density
blue enough to abolish the stars.
As long as the rainbow lasts
the company stays.

Of black there is never enough.

One by one the lights in the house go out.
Step over the threshold. Forget
to take my hand.

Path

Aged by rains,
cool under pulsing trees,
the summer path is paved with winter leaves.
Roots lace it like an old man's veins.

And nothing in field, on hill, can so appal
burnt August and its transitory walker
as this which leads a summer
towards its fall.

Now under cover
of the leopard pelt
of that lean way, more heat, more passion's felt
than ever in shimmering field by usual lover.

Fanged with surprising light, the path means harm.
Not calm, not comfort, not release at last.
White innocent motes of dust
rise up and swarm.

Between

The wet and weight of this half-born English winter
is not the weather of those fragmentary half-true willows
that break in the glass of the canal behind our rudder
as water arrives in our wake—a travelling arrow
of now, of now, of now. Leaves of the water

furl back from our prow, and as the pinnate narrow
seam of where we are drives through the mirror
of where we have to be, alder and willow
double crookedly, reverse, assume a power
to bud out tentatively in gold and yellow,
so it looks as if what should be end of summer—
seeds, dead nettles, berries, naked boughs—
is really the anxious clouding of first spring.
. . . 'Real' is what water is imagining.

The Circle

It is imagination's white face remembers
snow, its shape, a fluted shell on shoot
or flower, its weight, the permanence of winter
pitched against the sun's absolute root.

All March is shambles, shards. Yet no amber
chestnut, Indian, burnished by its tent
cuts to a cleaner centre or keeps summer
safer in its sleep. Ghost be content.

You died in March when white air hurt the maples.
Birches knelt under ice. Roads forgot
their way in aisles of frost. There were no petals.

Face, white face, you are snow in the green hills.
High stones complete your circle where trees start.
Granite and ice are colours of the heart.

The Sun Appears in November

When trees are bare,
when ground is more glowing than summer,
in sun, in November,
you can see what lay under
confusing eloquence of green.

Bare boughs in their cunning
twist this way and that way,
trying to persuade with crooked reasoning.
But trees are constrained from within
to conform to skeleton.

Nothing they put on
will equal these lines of cold branches,
the willows in bunches,
birches like lightning,
transparent in brown spinneys, beeches.

Meniscus

The moon at its two extremes,
promise and reminiscence,
future and past succeeding each other,
the rim of a continuous event.

These eyes which contain the moon
in the suspect lens of an existence,
guiding it from crescent to crescent
as from mirror to distorting mirror.

The good bones sheathed in my skin,
the remarkable knees and elbows
working without audible complaint
in the salty caves of their fitting.

My cup overfilled at the brim
and beyond the belief of the brim,
absolved by the power of the lip
from the necessity of falling.

The Price

The fear of loneliness, the wish
to be alone;
love grown rank as seeding grass
in every room,
and anger at it raging at it,
storming it down.

Also that four-walled chrysalis
and impediment, home;
that lamp and hearth, that easy fit
of bed to bone;
those children, too, sharp witnesses
of all I've done.

My dear, the ropes that bind us
are safe to hold;
the walls that crush us
keep us from the cold.
I know the price, and still
I pay it, pay it:

Words, their furtive kiss,
illicit gold.

If I Could Paint Essences

(*Hay on Wye*)

Another day in March. Late
rawness and wetness. I hear my mind say,
if only I could paint essences.

Such as the mudness of mud
on this rainsoaked dyke where coltsfoot
displays its yellow misleading daisy.

Such as the westness of west here
in England's last thatched, rivered
county. Red ploughland. Green pasture.

Black cattle. Quick water. Overpainted
by lightshafts from layered gold
and purple cumulus. A cloudness of clouds

which are not like anything but clouds.

But just as I arrive at true sightness of seeing,
unexpectedly I want to play on those bell-toned
cellos of delicate not-quite-flowering larches

that offer, on the opposite hill, their unfurled
amber instruments—floating, insubstantial, a rising
horizon of music embodied in light.

And in such imagining I lose sight of sight.
Just as I'll lose the tune of what
hurls in my head, as I turn back, turn

home to you, conversation, the inescapable ache
of trying to catch, say, the catness of cat
as he crouches, stalking his shadow,

on the other side of the window.

Small Philosophical Poem

Dr Animus, whose philosophy is a table,
sits down contentedly to a square meal.
The plates lie there, and there,
just where they should lie.
His feet stay just where they should stay,
between legs and the floor.
His eyes believe the clean waxed surfaces
are what they are.

But while he's eating his un-
exceptional propositions, his wise
wife, Anima, sweeping a haze-gold decanter
from a metaphysical salver,
pours him a small glass of doubt.
Just what he needs.
He smacks his lips and cracks his knuckles.
The world is the pleasure of thought.

He'd like to stay awake all night
(elbows on the table)
talking of how the table might not be there.
But Anima, whose philosophy is hunger,
perceives the plates are void in empty air.
The floor is void beneath his trusting feet.
Peeling her glass from its slender cone of fire,
she fills the room with love. And fear. And fear.

Ah Babel

your tower allures me—
its lettered battlements,
sounds, words,
but the high forehead unfinished.

I would desert my eyes
for the windows that are you.

Your multiple stones
despise clouds.
Your country's bleached sand
and black scars

lead to a sky
as clean as meaning.

Nameless
in mist and silence,
grey against grey,
I exist in your promise,

praise you for this present
of a vast home,
pronounced ruin,
all that is known.

Swifts

Spring comes little, a little. All April it rains.
The new leaves stick in their fists; new ferns still
        fiddleheads.
But one day the swifts are back. Face to the sun like a
        child
You shout, 'The swifts are back!'

Sure enough, bolt nocks bow to carry one sky-scyther
Two hundred miles an hour across fullblown windfields.
Swereee swereee. Another. And another.
It's the cut air falling in shrieks on our chimneys and
     roofs.

The next day, a fleet of high crosses cruises in ether.
These are the air pilgrims, pilots of air rivers.
But a shift of wing, and they're earth-skimmers, daggers
Skilful in guiding the throw of themselves away from
     themselves.

Quick flutter, a scimitar upsweep, out of danger of
     touch, for
Earth is forbidden to them, water's forbidden to them,
All air and fire, little owlish ascetics, they outfly storms,
They rush to the pillars of altitude, the thermal
     fountains.

Here is a legend of swifts, a parable—
When the Great Raven bent over earth to create the
     birds,
The swifts were ungrateful. They were small muddy
     things
Like shoes, with long legs and short wings,

So they took themselves off to the mountains to sulk.
And they stayed there. 'Well,' said the Raven, after years
     of this,
'I will give you the sky. You can have the whole sky
On condition that you give up rest.'

'Yes, yes,' screamed the swifts, 'We abhor rest.
We detest the filth of growth, the sweat of sleep,
Soft nests in the wet fields, slimehold of worms.
Let us be free, be air!'

So the Raven took their legs and bound them into their
        bodies.
He bent their wings like boomerangs, honed them like
        knives.
He streamlined their feathers and stripped them of
        velvet.
Then he released them, *Never to Return*

Inscribed on their feet and wings. And so
We have swifts, though in reality, not parables but
Bolts in the world's need: swift
Swifts, not in punishment, not in ecstasy, simply

Sleepers over oceans in the mill of the world's breathing.
The grace to say they live in another firmament.
A way to say the miracle will not occur,
And watch the miracle.

Himalayan Balsam

Orchid-lipped, loose-jointed, purplish, indolent flowers,
with a ripe smell of peaches, like a girl's breath through
        lipstick,
delicate and coarse in the weedlap of late summer rivers,
dishevelled, weak-stemmed, common as brambles, as
        love which

subtracts us from seasons, their courtships and murders,
(*Meta segmentata* in her web, and the male waiting,
between blossom and violent blossom, meticulous
    spiders
repeated in gossamer, and the slim males waiting).

Fragrance too rich for keeping, too light to remember,
like grief for the cat's sparrow and the wild gull's
beach-hatched embryo. (She ran from the reaching
    water
with the broken egg in her hand, but the clamped bill

refused brandy and grubs, a shred too naked and
    perilous for
life, offered freely in cardboard boxes, little windowsill
coffins for bird death, kitten death, squirrel death,
    summer
repeated and ended in heartbreak, in sad small funerals.)

Sometimes, shaping bread or scraping potatoes for
    supper,
I have stood in the kitchen, transfixed by what I'd call
    love,
if love were a whiff, a wanting for no particular lover,
no child, or baby, or creature. 'Love, dear love,'

I could cry to these scent-spilling ragged flowers,
and mean nothing but 'no', in that word's breath,
to their evident going, their important descent through
    red towering
stalks to the riverbed. It's not, as I thought, that death

creates love. More that love knows death. Therefore
tears, therefore poems, therefore long stone sobs of
    cathedrals
that speak to no ferret or fox, that prevent no massacre.
(I am combing abundant leaves from these icy shallows.)

Love, it was you who said, 'Murder the killer
we have to call life and we'd be a bare planet under a
    dead sun.'
Then I loved you with the usual soft lust of October
that says 'yes' to the coming winter and a summoning
    odour of balsam.

The Fish Are All Sick

The fish are all sick, the great whales dead,
The villages stranded in stone on the coast,
Ornamental, like pearls on the fringe of a coat.
Sea men who knew what the ocean did,
Turned their low houses away from the surf.
But new men, who come to be rural and safe,
Add big glass views and begonia beds.

Water keeps to itself.
White lip after lip
Curls to a close on the littered beach.
Something is sicker and blacker than fish.
And closing its grip, and closing its grip.

In the Tunnel of Summers

Moving from day into day,
I don't know how,
eating these plums now
this morning for breakfast,
tasting of childhood's
mouth-pucker tartness,
watching the broad light
seed in the fences,
honey of barley,
gold ocean, grasses,
as the tunnel of summers,
of nothing but summers,
opens again
in my travelling senses.

I am eight and eighteen and eighty
all the Augusts of my day.

Why should I be, I be
more than another?
Brown foot in sandal,
burnt palm on flaked clay,
flesh under waterfall
baubled in strong spray,
blood on the stubble
of fly-sweet hay.
Why not my mother's, my
grandmother's ankle
hurting as harvest hurts

thistle and animal?
A needle of burning;
why this way or that way?

They are already building the long straw cemetery
where my granddaughter's daughter has been born and
buried.

Waving to Elizabeth

(*for Elizabeth Bishop*)

For mapmakers' reasons, the transcontinental air routes
must have been diverted today, and Sunderland's
        stratosphere
is being webbed over by shiny, almost invisible spider jets
creeping with deliberate intention on the skin-like air,
each suspended from the chalky silk of its passing.
        Thready at first,
as if written by two, four, fine felt nibs, the lines become
        cloudy
as the planes cease to need them. In freedom they
        dissolve. Just
as close observation dissipates in the wind of theory.

Eight or nine of them now, all writing at once,
rising from the south on slow rails, slow arcs, an armillary
prevented by air from completing its evidence,
unravelling instead in soft, powdery stripes, which
        seem to be

the only clouds there are between what's simply here as
    park,
house, roof, road, cars, etcetera, and the wide, long view
they must have of us there, if they bother to look.
They have taken so much of us up with them, too:

Money and newspapers, meals, toilets, old films, hot
    coffee.
Yet the miles between us, though measurable, seem unreal.
I have to think, 'Here it is, June 19th, 1983.
I'm waving from a waste patch by the Thornhill School.'
As perhaps you think back from your trip through the
    cosmos,
'Here where I love, it is no time at all. The geography
looks wonderful! This high, smooth sea's more quiet
    than the map is,
though the map, relieved of mapmakers, looks
    imprisoned and free.'

After the Fall

Adam: Lady,
    I've not had a moment's love
    since I was expelled.
    Let me in.

Eve: Lord,
    I've not had a moment's rest
    since I was a rib.
    Put me back.

Two Poems for Frances Horovitz (1938-83):

Red Rock Fault

This is the South-West wind
the North-East breathes and knows;
that lifts linoleum under kitchen doors,
that bends thorned trees one way on the moors,
that hooks back little white knots of the Irthing
in shaggy impermanent weirs
by the empty farm at the river's turning
where spiders make nets for the silted windows
and machinery rusts in the byres.
Fran, has it been two years?

I see you again in your boy's coat
on that sudden and slithery hill of stones
where we ducked from the wind one afternoon
when slant light cut and shone
through glass-white arcs of October grass.
It was just by the Red Rock Fault
where limestone meets sandstone, lass.
You carried your love of that rushy place
in the candle of your living face
to set in the dark of your poems.

And now we have only the poems.
While snow-light, water-light winters still
will come to that ridge of Roman stones,
Spadeadam, Birdoswald, high Whin Sill,
where so many trees lose uncountable leaves
to this wind—one breath from uncountable lives.
Shrill clouds of gathering jackdaws, starlings,
storm an enormous sky.
That huge split ash by the ruined steading—
Cocidius, life-keeper, live eye.

Willow Song

I went down to the railway
But the railway wasn't there.
A long scar lay across the waste
Bound up with vetch and maidenhair
And birdsfoot trefoils everywhere.
But the clover and the sweet hay,
The cranesbill and the yarrow
Were as nothing to the rose bay
    the rose bay, the rose bay,
As nothing to the rose bay willow.

I went down to the river
But the river wasn't there.
A hill of slag lay in its course
With pennycress and cocklebur
And thistles bristling with fur.

But ragweed, dock and bitter may
and hawkbit in the hollow
Were as nothing to the rose bay,
    the rose bay, the rose bay
As nothing to the rose bay willow.

I went down to find my love.
My sweet love wasn't there.
A shadow stole into her place
And spoiled the loosestrife of her hair
And counselled me to pick despair.
Old elder and young honesty
Turned ashen, but their sorrow
Was as nothing to the rose bay
    the rose bay, the rose bay,
As nothing to the rose bay willow.

O I remember summer
When the hemlock was in leaf.
The sudden poppies by the path
Were little pools of crimson grief.
Sick henbane cowered like a thief.
But self-heal sprang up in her way,
And mignonette's light yellow,
To flourish with the rose bay,
    the rose bay, the rose bay,
To flourish with the rose bay willow.

Its flames took all the wasteland
And all the river's silt,
But as my dear grew thin and grey

They turned as white as salt or milk.
Great purples withered out of guilt,
And bright weeds blew away
In cloudy wreaths of summer snow.
And the first one was the rose bay,
      the rose bay, the rose bay,
The first one was the rose bay willow.

Dreaming of the Dead

(*i.m. Anne Pennington*)

I believe, but what is belief?

I receive the forbidden dead.
They appear in the mirrors of asleep
To accuse or be comforted.

All the selves of myself they keep,
From a bodiless time arrive,
Retaining in face and shape

Shifting lineaments of alive.
So whatever it is you are,
Dear Anne, bent smilingly grave

Over wine glasses filled by your fire,
Is the whole of your life you gave
To our fictions of what you were.

Not a shadow of you can save
These logs that crackle with light,
Or this smoky image I have—

Your face at the foot of a flight
Of wrought-iron circular stairs.
I am climbing alone in the night

Among stabbing, unmerciful flares.
Oh, I am what I see and know,
But no other solid thing's there

Except for the terrible glow
Of your face and its quiet belief,
Light wood ash falling like snow

On my weaker grief.

The Fiction Makers

(*i.m. Frances Horovitz*)

We were the wrecked elect,
the ruined few. Youth,
youth, the Café Iruña
and the bullfight set,
looped on Lepanto brandy
but talking 'truth'.
Hem, the 4 a.m. wisecrack,
the hard way in,

that story we were all at the end of
and couldn't begin—
we thought we were living now
but we were living then.

Sanctified Pound, a knot
of nerves in his fist,
squeezing the Goddamn iamb
out of our verse,
making it new in his
archaeological plot—
to maintain 'the sublime'
in the factive? Couldn't be done.
Something went wrong
with 'new' in the Pisan pen;
he thought he was making now,
but he was making then.

Virginia, Vanessa,
a teapot, a Fitzroy fuss,
'Semen?' asks Lytton,
eyeing a smudge on a dress.
How to educate England
and keep a correct address
on the path to the river through
Auschwitz? Belsen?
Auden and Isherwood
stalking glad boys in Berlin—
they thought they were suffering now
but they were suffering then.

Out of pink-cheeked Cwmdonkin,
Dylan with his Soho grin.
Planted in the fiercest of flames,
gold ash on a stem.
When Henry jumped out of his joke,
Mr Bones sat in.
Even you, with your breakable heart
in your ruined skin,
those poems all written
that have to be you, dear friend,
you guessed you were dying now,
but you were dying then.

Here is a table with glasses,
ribbed cages tipped back,
or turned on a hinge to each other
to talk, to talk,
mouths that are drinking or smiling
or quoting some book,
or laughing out laughter as candletongues
lick at the dark.
So bright in this fiction
forever becoming its end,
we think we are laughing now,
but we are laughing then.

Making Poetry

'You have to inhabit poetry
if you want to make it.'

And what's 'to inhabit'?

To be in the habit of, to wear
words, sitting in the plainest light,
in the silk of morning, in the shoe of night;
a feeling bare and frondish in surprising air;
familiar . . . rare.

And what's 'to make'?

To be and to become words' passing
weather; to serve a girl on terrible
terms, embark on voyages over voices,
evade the ego-hill, the misery-well,
the siren hiss of *publish, success, publish,
success, success, success.*

And why inhabit, make, inherit poetry?

Oh, it's the shared comedy of the worst
blessed; the sound leading the hand;
a wordlife running from mind to mind
through the washed rooms of the simple senses;
one of those haunted, undefendable, unpoetic
crosses we have to find.

A Dream of Stones

(*for Norman Nicholson*)

I dreamed a summer's labour,
loss or discovery,
had brought me, on the sand,
to a nest of stones.
What shall I do with these stones
that shine too weakly to be gems,
that might be seeds?

Stones are to build with,
but here there is tidal sea,
bare sand and sea.

Why, since these stones
look anxious to be used,
should they not be planted?
There are no trees here.
Maybe there are trees
coiled inside the smoothness
of the stone seeds.

I am pocking the soil with my heel:
here, here, here, here.
Into each footprint, a glimmering pearl.

They will not be counted,
these seeds, these hopes, these
possible offerings from impossible language.
They resist being tears.

I tell them to you now
as if they were gifts
too alive to be left unburied
under common years.

Trinity at Low Tide

Sole to sole with your reflection
   on the glassy beach,
your shadow gliding beside you,
   you stride in triplicate across the sand.
Waves, withdrawn to limits on their leash,
   are distant, repetitious whisperings,
while doubling you, the rippling tideland
      deepens you.

Under you, transparent yet exact,
   your downward ghost keeps pace—
pure image, cleansed of human overtones:
   a travelling sun, your face;
your breast, a field of sparkling shells and stones.
   All blame is packed into that black, featureless
third trick of light that copies you
      and cancels you.

Salter's Gate

There, in that lost
    corner of the ordnance survey.
Drive through the vanity—
    two pubs and a garage—of Satley,
then right, cross the A68
    past down-at-heel farms and a quarry,

you can't miss it, a 'T' instead of a 'plus'
    where the road meets a wall.
If it's a usual day
    there'll be freezing wind, and you'll
stumble climbing the stile
    (a ladder, really) as you pull

your hat down and zip up your jacket.
    Out on the moor,
thin air may be strong enough to
    knock you over,
but if you head into it
    downhill, you can shelter

in the wide, cindery trench of an old
    leadmine-to-Consett railway.
You may have to share it
    with a crowd of dirty
supercilious-looking ewes, who will baaa
    and cut jerkily away

after posting you blank stares
    from their foreign eyes.
One winter we came across five
    steaming, icicle-hung cows.
But in summer, when the heather's full of nests,
    you'll hear curlews

following you, raking your memory, maybe,
    with their cries;
or, right under your nose,
    a grouse will whirr up surprised,
like a poet startled by a line
    when it comes to her sideways.

No protection is offered by trees—
    Hawthorn the English call May,
a few struggling birches.
    But of wagtails and yellowhammers, plenty,
and peewits who never say *peewit*,
    more a minor, *go'way, go'way*.

Who was he, Salter? Why was this his gate?
    A pedlars' way, they carried
salt to meat. The place gives tang to
    survival, its unstoppable view,
a reservoir, ruins of the lead mines, new
    forestry pushing from the right, the curlew.

Cold

Snow. No roofs this morning, alps, ominous message
     for the jackdaws prospecting maps of melt.
Something precipitates an avalanche.

A tablecloth slips off noisily
     pouring heavy laundry into detergent,
a basin of virgin textiles, pocked distinctively

with crystals. Your shovel violates this *blanchissage*
     with useful bustle, urgency
pretends, helpless as the swallowed road on which

the air lets fall again a lacier
organza snow-veil. Winter bridal
the muffled dog fouls briefly. *Don't the cedars*

look beautiful, bent under clouds of fall?
And it's true, time has no pull
on us; we set it aside for another

'very serious and fundamental' briefing:
chaffinches at the birdfeed, a sentinel
jackdaw on exposed slates, worried men

tiptoeing their accelerators, deepening
very carefully each other's ruts.
As if—for how long?—matter had beaten them

and the cold were bowing them back to—
or forward to—a steadier state. Ice
sets in and verifies the snow.

Imagine a hidden rule, escaped from words,
stealing the emergency away from us,
starving the animals eventually; first, the birds.

Washing the Clocks

Time to go to school, cried
the magnifying lens of the alarm clock.
Time to go home now, the school's
Latin numerals decided.

Days into weeks, months into years.

It's time now thoroughly to wash
the outsides and insides of the clocks.

The broken clocks line up along the dresser,
worn out, submitting patiently.
An old woman in a yellow head-square
prepares to take them apart.

First she pries the glass off a black clock.
The glow-painted arabics fade as she scrubs.

Next, with a little lead key, she
applies herself to a school clock.

Tears must have rusted the hinge.
She has to force the case open.
Two pointed swords and a needle
clatter to the tessellated floor.

Where have they gone? Look for them.
Feel for the hands in the dust,
in the blowing sand. Finger by finger
the numerals break off and drop down.

How competently she's removing
the scarred blank face of my old school clock.

Behind it, the whirring machine,
gleaming brass rods and revolving cogs
making up time by themselves,
rinsing the mesh of their wheels in mysterious oil.

Politesse

A memory kissed my mind
   and its courtesy hurt me.
On an ancient immaculate lawn
   in an English county
you declared love, but from *politesse*
   didn't inform me
that the fine hairs shadowing my lip
   were a charge against me.

Your hair was gods' gold, curled,
   and your cricketer's body
tanned—as mine never would tan—
   when we conquered Italy
in an Austin 7 convertible,
   nineteen thirty;
I remember its frangible spokes
   and the way you taught me

to pluck my unsightly moustache
   with a tool you bought me.
I bought us a sapphire, flawed,
   (though you did repay me)
from a thief on the Ponte Vecchio.
   Good breeding made me
share the new tent with Aileen
   while you and Hartley,

in the leaky, unpatchable other,
   were dampened nightly.
If I weren't *virgo intacta*,
   you told me sternly,
you'd take me like a cat in heat
   and never respect me.
That was something I thought about
   constantly, deeply,

in the summer of '54, when I
   fell completely
for a Milanese I only met once
   while tangoing, tipsy,

on an outdoor moon-lit dance-floor.
    I swear you lost me
when he laid light fingers on my lips
    and then, cat-like, kissed me.

Bloody Bloody

Who I am? You tell me
first who you are,
that's manners. And don't shout.
I can hear perfectly well.

Oh. A psychologist.
So you think I'm mad.

Ah, just unhappy.

You must be stupid if you
think it's mad to be unhappy.
Is that what they teach you
at university these days?

I'm sure you're bloody clever.

Bloody? A useful word.
What would *you* say, jolly?

It's bloody bloody,
I assure you,
having to sit up
for a psychiatrist—
sorry, *behavioural psychologist*,
I know there's a difference—
when I want to
lie down and sleep.

The only sensible thing,
at my age, is to be
as you well know
dead, but since they
can't or won't manage
anything like that here,
I consider my right to sleep
to be bloody sacred.

I can't hear you,
I'm closing my eyes.

Please don't open the curtains.

I said *keep the curtains shut!*
Thank you.
            Hate you?
Of course I hate you,
but I can't, in honesty,
say I blame you.
You have to do your job.

There.
That's my telephone.
How fortunate.
You'll avail yourself
of this opportunity, won't you,
to slip tactfully away.

Hello? Yes,
two pieces of good news.
One,
you've just interrupted a most
unnecessary visit,
a young psychological person
is seeing herself out.
Two,
you'll be relieved
to hear I'm worse, much worse.

Black Hole

I have grown small
inside my house of words,
empty and hard,
pebble rattling in a shell.

People around me, people.
Maybe I know them.
All so young
and cloudy, not . . . not real.

I can't help being the hole
I've fallen into.
Wish I could tell you
how I feel.

Heavy as mud, bowels
sucking at my head.
I'm being digested.
Remember those moles,

lawn full of them in April,
piles of earth they threw
out of their tunnels. Me, too.
Me, too. That's how I'll

be remembered. Piles
of words, sure, to show
where I was. But nothing true
about me left, child.

Lost

Stone-age, stone-grey eyes
clear in her glove-like skin;
a look of having been ironed
before she shuffled in.

Cradling a pink blonde doll
in a quilted bag, pink satin.
She lifts it out a while,
she puts it back again.

Her dead child? Poor, poor lady.
We burn to know . . . *what reason?*
No sign, from mouth or body.
She stuns our pity, even.

Journal Entry: Impromptu in C Minor

(*Edinburgh, October 1988*)

After weeks of October drench,
a warm orange day,
a conflagration of all the trees and streets in Edinburgh.

Let me have no thoughts
in this weather of pure sensation.

Getting into the car is a coatless sensation.
Driving through the traffic
is the feeling of falling leaves.

The Firth, like the sky, is blue, blue,
with sandy brown puffs of surf on the oily beaches.
The sea swell rises and spills,
rises and spills, tumbling its load of crockery
without breakage.

Is a metaphor a thought?
Then let these shells be shells,
these sharp white sails be sails.

Today the pink enormous railway bridge
is neither a three-humped camel nor a dinosaur
but a grand feat of Scottish engineering;
now and then it rumbles peacefully
as a tiny train, rather embarrassed, scuttles across it.

Sitting with pure sensation on the breakwater,
I unhook the wires of my mind.
I undo the intellectual spider's web.

Then I correct myself.
Soon I'm standing in my grid of guilts
hastily reaching for my thoughts.

For there are people out there.
Not abstractions, not ideas, but people.
In the black, beyond the blue of my perception,
in the huge vault where the wires won't reach,
the dead are lively.
The moment I take off my thought-clothes
I expose every nerve to their waves.

What is this sad marching melody?
A spy, a column on reconnaissance,
the theme from Schubert's Impromptu in C Minor.

It is 1943.
In a frame house that has forgotten him,
a dead man is playing the piano.
I am ten years old. For the first time
I watch a grown woman weep.
Her husband, the white-haired Jewish philosopher,
makes shy mistakes in English.
He puts an arm around his wife
and bows his head.

The theme returns years later
to a farmhouse in Vermont.
This time I myself am at the piano,
a puzzled girl I instantly recognise
although she died through more years than Schubert
    lived
to make room for the woman I am now.

I smile at her ambition.
She doesn't yet know she will be deaf.

She doesn't yet know how deaf she's been.

What is the matter?

This is the matter: deafness and deadness.
The shoe-heaps, hills of fillings, children's bones.
Headlines blacking out the breakfast chatter
    (We go on eating).
Static and foreign voices on the radio
    (We are late for school).

Then silence folding us in,
folding them under.

But here is the melody.

And here, 'our daemonic century'
in which a dead man's dead march
plays itself over and over
on a fine fall day in South Queensferry
in the head of a fortunate (though deaf) American
    grandmother.

She sits in the momentary sun looking at the sea.

Once there lived in Austria a schoolmaster's son,
shy, myopic, a little stout, but lucky,
for his talent was exactly suited to his time.
Careless of his health in an age of medical ignorance,
he died at thirty-one, probably of syphilis.
A few moments of his life, five notes of it,
fuse with a few impromptu responses,
a few contemporary cells.

They provide the present and future
of an every-minute dying planet
with a helix, a hinge of survival.

Letter to Sylvia Plath

(Grantchester, May 1988)

They are great healers, English springs.
You loved their delicate colourings—
sequential yellows, eggshell blues—
not pigments you preferred to use,
lady of pallors and foetal jars
and surgical interiors.
But wasn't it warmth you wanted most?

These Grantchester willows keep your ghost,
young and in love and half way through
the half-life that was left to you.
The Cam still crawls through patient grass,
preserving ephemerals in glass.
A bull thrush shouts from a willow thicket,
Catch it! Catch it! Catch it! Catch it!
Catch what? An owl in a petalled dress?
The gnarl at the root of a distress?

Dear Sylvia, we must close our book.
Three springs you've perched like a black rook
between sweet weather and my mind.
At last I have to seem unkind
and exorcise my awkward awe.
My shoulder doesn't like your claw.

Yet first, forgiveness. Let me shake
some echoes from old balled eyed Blake
over your grave and praise in rhyme
the fiercest poet of our time—

you with your outsized gift for joy
who did the winged life destroy,
and bought with death a mammoth name
to set in the cold museum of fame.

Your art was darkness. No, your art
was a gulping candle in the dark.
In the beginning was a curse:
a hag, a drowned man and a nurse
hid in the mirror of the moon
unquietly to work your doom.
A dissolute nun, you had to serve
the demon muse who peeled your nerve
and fuelled your energy with hate.

Malevolent will-power made you great,
while round you in the Sacred Wood
tall archetypal statues stood
rooted in air and in your mind.
The proud impossibles loomed behind,
pilasters buttressing a frieze
of marble, moonlit amputees.

Sylvia, I see you in this view
of glassy absolutes where you,
a frantic Alice, trip on snares,
crumple and drown in your own tears.
You were your cave of crippled dreams
and ineradicable screams,
and you were the pure gold honey bee
prisoned in poisonous jealousy.

The gratitude and love you thought
the world would give you if you fought
for all your tears could not be found
in reputation's building ground.
O give the mole an eagle's soul
and watch it battling in its hole.

Because you were selfish and sad and died,
we have grown up on the other side
of a famous girl you didn't know.
The future is where the dead go
in rage, bewilderment and pain
to make and magnify their name.

Meanwhile, the continuous present casts
longer reflections on the past.
Nothing has changed much. Famine, war
fatten your Spider as before.
Your hospital of bleeding parts
devours its haul of human hearts,
excreting what it cannot use
as celluloid or paper news;
eye for eye and tooth for tooth,
bomb for bomb and youth for youth.

Yet who would believe the colour green
had so many ways of being green?
In England, still, your poet's spring
arrives, unravelling everything.
A yellowhammer in the gorse
creates each minute's universe;
a blackbird singing from a thorn
is all the joy of being reborn.

Even in Heptonstall in May
the wind invites itself away,
leaving black stone to compromise
with stitchwort, dandelions and flies.
Tell me, do all those weeds and trees
strewing their cool longevities
over the garden of your bed
have time for you, now you are dead?

Behind the pricked-out drape of night
is there a sheet-white screen of light
where death meets birth to reconcile
the contradictions of your will?
Perfection is terrible, you said.
The perfect are barren, like the dead.

Yet life, more terrible, maunches on,
as blood-red light loops back at dawn,
seizing, devouring, giving birth
to the mass atrocity of the earth.
Poor Sylvia, could you not have been
a little smaller than a queen—
a river, not a tidal wave
engulfing all you tried to save?

Rather than not be justified
you sickened in loneliness and died,
while we live on in messy lives,
rueful or tired or barely wise.
Ageing, we labour to exist.
Beyond existence, nothing is.

Out of this world there is no source
of yellower rape or golder gorse,
nor in the galaxy higher place,
I think, for human mind or face.

We learn to be human when we kneel
to imagination, which is real
long after reality is dead
and history has put its bones to bed.
Sylvia, you have won at last,
embodying the living past,
catching the anguish of your age
in accents of a private rage.

The Other House

In the house of childhood
I looked up to my mother's face.
The sturdy roofbeam of her smile
Buckled the rooms in place.
A shape of the unchangeable
    taught me the word 'gone'.

In the house of growing up
I lined my prison wall
With lives I worshipped as I read.
If I chose one, I chose all,
Such paper clothes I coveted
    and ached to try on.

The house of youth has a grand door,
A ruin the other side
Where death watch & company
Compete with groom and bride.
Nothing was what seemed to be
    in that charged dawn.

They advertised the house of love,
I bought the house of pain,
With shabby little wrongs and rights
Where beams should have been.
How could those twisted, splintered nights
    stand up alone?

My angry house was a word house,
A city of the brain,
Where buried heads and salt gods
Struggled to breathe again.
Into those echoing, sealed arcades
    I hurled a song.

It glowed with an electric pulse,
Firing the sacred halls.
Bright reproductions of itself
Travelled the glassy walls.
Ignis fatuus, cried my voice,
    and I moved on.

I drove my mind to a strange house,
Infinitely huge and small:
The cone to which this dew-drop earth
Leeches, invisible.
Infinite steps of death and birth
    lead up and down.

Beneath me, infinitely deep,
Solidity dissolves.
Above me, infinitely wide,
Galactic winter sprawls.
That house of the utterly outside,
    became my home.

In it, the house of childhood
Safeguards my mother's face.
A lifted eyebrow's 'Yes, and so?'
Latches the rooms in place.
I tell my children all I know
    of the word 'gone'.

Elegy

Whenever my father was left with nothing to do—
    waiting for someone to 'get ready',
or facing the gap between graduate seminars
    and dull after-suppers in his study
grading papers or writing a review—
    he played the piano.

I think of him packing his lifespan
        carefully, like a good leather briefcase,
each irritating chore wrapped in floating passages
        for the left hand and right hand
by Chopin or difficult Schumann;
        nothing inside it ever rattled loose.

Not rationalism, though you could cut your tongue
        on the blade of his reasonable logic.
Only at the piano did he become
        the bowed, reverent, wholly absorbed Romantic.
The theme of his heroic, unfinished piano sonata
        could have been Brahms.

Boredom, or what he disapproved of as
        'sitting around with your mouth open'
oddly pursued him. He had small stamina.
        Whenever he succumbed to bouts of winter
                bronchitis,
the house sank a little into its snowed-up garden,
        missing its musical swim-bladder.

None of this suggests how natural he was.
        For years I thought fathers played the piano
just as dogs barked and babies grew.
        We children ran in and out of the house,
taking for granted that the 'Trout' or E flat Major
                Impromptu
        would be rippling around us.

For him, I think, playing was solo flying, a bliss
        of removal, of being alone.
Not happily always; never an escape,
        for he was affectionate, and the household hum
he pretended to find trivial or ridiculous
        daily sustained him.

When he talked about music, it was never
        of the *lachrimae rerum*
that trembled from his drawn-out phrasing
        as raindrops phrase themselves along a wire;
no, he defended movable doh or explained the amazing
        physics of the octave.

We'd come in from school and find him
        crossed-legged on the jungle of the floor,
guts from one of his Steinways strewn about him.
        He always got the pieces back in place.
I remember the yellow covers of Schirmer's Editions
        and the bound Peters Editions in the bookcase.

When he defected to the cello in later years
        Grandmother, *in excrucio*, mildly exclaimed,
'Wasn't it lovely when Steve liked to play the piano.'
        Now I'm the grandmother listening to Steve at the
        piano.
Lightly, in strains from the Brahms-Haydn variations,
        his audible image returns to my humming ears.

When the camel is dust it goes through the needle's eye

This hot summer wind
is tiring my mother.
It tires her to watch it
buffeting the poppies.
Down they bow
in their fluttering kimonos,
a suppressed populace,
an unpredictable dictator.

The silver-haired reeds
are also supplicants.
Stripped of its petals,
clematis looks grey
on the wall. My mother,
who never came here,
suggests it's too hot
to cook supper.

Her tiredness gets everywhere
like blown topsoil,
teasing my eyes and tongue,
wrinkling my skin.
Summer after summer, silt
becomes landfill between us,
level and walkable,
level, eventually, and simple.

Where the Animals Go

The beasts in Eden
cradle the returning souls of earth's animals.

The horse, limp cargo, craned down to the terrible quay,
is butchered into a heaven of his own hoofed kind.

The retriever mangled on the motorway, the shot
Alsatian by the sheepfold, the mutilated black-faced
        sheep—
they rise like steam, like cumulus, crowding in together,
each into the haunches of its archetype.

The drowned vole, the pheasant brought down with his
        fires,
the kitten in the jacket of its panicking fleas,
flying souls, furred, feathered, scaled, shelled, streaming
upward, upward through the wide thoughtless rose
        empyrean.

God absorbs them neatly in his green teeming cells.

There, sexed as here, they're without hurt or fear.
Heaven is honeycombed with their arrivals and entries.
Two of each butterfly. Two of each beetle.
A great cowness sways on her full uddered way.
All kinds of cat watch over the hive like churches.
Their pricked ears, pinnacles. Their gold eyes, windows.

As I Lay Sleeping

(*for Carol Rumens*)

Out of the afterlife behind my eyelids
Arrived the offer of a plush hotel.
Yes, there it was, as we were driven past it,
High on a green embankment, white and big.
It had to be Russian. Where else does marble curl
In tufted layers like a powdered wig?
Geraniums blazed in tubs and hanging baskets.
Not for us. We had too many kids,

But where? I'd swear I was alone with you.
The sun set in some oil-polluted stream,
And we were floating there or wading through
Its tessellated fragments when the dream
Revealed the awful place assigned to us:
An eighteen-storey highrise with a view
Into a gulf or gullet—an immense abyss.
The children crowded to the edge of this,

Then one by one they held their hands together,
The way you hold them out to dive or pray,
And off they peeled. One body, then another,
The little stony fledglings fell away.
A dream, I thought, I shouldn't be afraid.
Why was I sure the truth would be more
Beautiful and lethal? Was it war?
No, it was only daylight. But it stayed.

Saying the World

The way you say the world is what you get.
What's more, you haven't time to change or choose.
The words swim out to pin you in their net

Before you guess you're in the TV set,
Lit up and sizzling in unfriendly news.
The mind's machine—and you invented it—

Grinds out the formulae you have to fit,
The ritual syllables you need to use
To charm the world and not be crushed by it.

This cluttered motorway, that screaming jet,
Those crouching skeletons whose eyes accuse;
O see and say them, make yourself forget

The world is vaster than the alphabet,
And profligate, and meaner than the muse.
A bauble in the universe? Or shit?

Whichever way, you say the world you get.
Though what there is is always there to lose.
No crimson name redeems the poisoned rose.
The absolute's irrelevant. And yet . . .

(1994)

Vertigo

Mind led body
to the edge of the precipice.
They stared in desire
at the naked abyss.
If you love me, said mind,
take that step into silence.
If you love me, said body,
turn and exist.

A Surprise on the First Day of School

They give you a desk with a lid, mother.
They let you keep your book.
My desk's next to the window.
I can see the trees.
But you mustn't look out the window
    at light on the leaves.
You must look at the book.

A nice-smelling, shiny book, mother,
With words in it and pictures.
I mostly like the pictures,
    some of them animals and birds.
But you musn't look at the pictures.
You don't *ever* read the pictures.
You read the words!

Arioso Dolente

(*for my grandchildren when they become grandparents*)

A mother, who read and thought and poured herself into
    me;
she was the jug and I was the two-eared cup.
How she would scorn today's 'show-biz inanity,
democracy twisted, its high ideals sold up!'
       Cancer filched her voice, then cut her throat.
         Why is it
    none of the faces in this family snapshot
        looks upset?

A father, who ran downstairs as I practised the piano;
barefooted, buttoning his shirt, he shouted 'G,
D-natural, C-*flat*! *Dolente, arioso.*
Put all the griefs of the world in that change of key.'
     Who then could lay a finger on his sleeve
       to distress him with
  'One day, Steve, two of your well-taught daughters
       will be deaf.'

Mother must be sitting, left, on the porch-set,
you can just see her. My sister's on her lap.
And that's Steve confiding to his cigarette
something my mother's mother has to laugh at.
     The screened door twangs, slamming
       on its sprung hinge.
  Paint blisters on the steps; iced tea, grasscuttings,
     elm flowers, mock orange . . .

A grand June evening, like this one, not too buggy,
unselfquestioning midwestern, maybe 1951.
And, of course, there in my grandmother's memory
lives just such another summer—1890 or 91.
              Though it's not on her mind now/then.
                    No, she's thinking of
          the yeast-ring rising in the oven. Or how *any* shoes
                 irritate her bunion.

Paper gestures, pictures, newsprint laughter.
And after the camera winks and makes its catch,
the decibels drain away *for ever and ever.*
No need to say 'Look!' to these smilers on the porch,
              'Grandmother will have her stroke,
                    and you, mother, will nurse her.'
Or to myself, this woman died paralysed-dumb,
          and that one dumb from cancer.
Sufficient unto the day . . . Grandmother, poor and
          liturgical,
whose days were duties, stitches in the tea-brown
          blanket
she for years crocheted, its zigzag of yellow wool,
her grateful offering, her proof of goodness to present,
          gift-wrapped, to Our Father in Heaven. 'Accept,
              O Lord, this best-I-can-make-it soul.'
    And He: 'Thou good and faithful servant, lose thyself
                    and be whole.'

Consciousness walks on tiptoe through what happens.
So much is felt, so little of it said.
But ours is the breath on which the past depends.
'What happened' is what the living teach the dead,
who, smilingly lost to their lost concerns,
in grey on grey,
are all of them deaf, blind, unburdened
by today.

As if our recording selves, our mortal identities,
could be cupped in a concave universe or lens,
ageless at all ages, cleansed of memories,
not minding that meaningful genealogy extends
no further than mind's flash images reach back.
As for what happens next,
let all the griefs of the world
find keys for that.

Arioso dolente: from Beethoven's piano sonata, opus 110,
third movement; introduction to the fugue.

Moonrise

While my anxiety stood phoning you last evening,
My simpler self lay marvelling through glass
At the full moon marbling the clouds, climbing
In shafts, a headlamp through an underpass,
Until it swung free, cratered, deadly clear,
Earth's stillborn twin unsoiled by life or air.

And while our voices huddled mouth to ear,
I watched tenacity of long imagination
Cast her again in a film of the old goddess,
Chaste of the chase, more virgin than the Virgin,
Lifting herself from that rucked, unfeeling waste
As from the desert of her own ruined face.

Such an unhinging light. To see her. To see that.
As no one else had seen her. Or might see that.

Skills

Like threading a needle by computer, to align
the huge metal-plated tracks of the macadam-spreader
with two frail ramps to the plant-carrier.
Working alone on Sunday, overtime,
the driver powers the wheel: forward, reverse, forward
centimetre by centimetre . . . stop!

He leaps from the cab, a carefree Humphrey Bogart,
to check both sides. The digger sits up front
facing backwards at an angle to the flat,
its diplodocus-neck chained to a steel scaffold.
Its head fits neatly in the macadam-spreader's lap.
Satisfying. All of a piece and tightly wrapped.

Before he slams himself, whistling, into his load,
he eyes all six, twelve, eighteen, twenty-four tires.
Imagine a plane ascending. Down on the road,
this clever Matchbox toy that takes apart
grows small, now smaller still and more compact,
a crawling speck on the unfolding map.

An Angel

After a long drive west into Wales,
as I lay on my bed, waiting
for my mind to seep back through my body,
I watched two gothic panels draw apart.
Between them loomed an angel,
tall as a caryatid, wingless,
draped like Michelangelo's sibyl.
Never have I felt so profoundly looked into.

She was bracing on her hip an immense book
that at first I took for a Bible. Then
prickling consciousness seemed to apprehend
The Recording Angel.
The pen she wielded writhed like a caduceus,
and on the book
ECCE LIBER MORI had been branded.

This book she held out towards me,
arm-muscles tensing, but even as I reached
I knew it was too heavy to hold.
Its gravity, she made me feel, would crush me,
a black hole of infinitely compressed time.
Each page weighed as much as the world.

Drawing my attention to a flaw in the book's crust—
a glazed porthole, a lens of alizarin—
she focused it (it must have been a microscope)
and silently motioned me to look.
Fire folding fire was all I saw. Then the red glass

cleared and a blizzard of swimming cells
swept underneath it, lashing their whip-like tails,
clashing, fusing, consuming each other greedily,
fountaining into polyps and underwater flowers.
Soon—fast-forward—forests were shooting up.
Seasons tamed lagoons of bubbling mud
where, hatching from the scum, animalculae
crawled, swarmed, multiplied, disbanded,
swarmed again, raised cities out of dust,
destroyed them, died. I turned to the angel,
'Save these species,' I cried.
And brought my face right down on her book,
my cheek on the lens like a lid.

Instantly I knew I had put out a light
that had never been generated by a book.
That vision-furnace, that blink into genesis?
Nothing but a passing reflection of the angel.

Rising, for the first time afraid,
I confronted her immortality
circling like a bracelet of phosphorus
just outside the windscreen of the car.
For it seems I was still driving.
Solidity and substance disappeared.
A noose of frenzied, shimmering electrons,
motes of an approaching migraine,
closed around me.
And through that fluorescent manacle,
the road flowed on through Wales.

Granny Scarecrow

Tears flowed at the chapel funeral,
more beside the grave on the hill. Nevertheless,
after the last autumn ploughing,
they crucified her old flowered print housedress
live, on a pole.

Marjorie and Emily, shortcutting to school,
used to pass and wave; mostly Gran would wave back.
Two white Sunday gloves
flapped good luck from the crossbar; her head's plastic sack
would nod, as a rule.

But when winter arrived, her ghost thinned.
The dress began to look starved in its field of snowcorn.
One glove blew off and was lost.
The other hung blotchy with mould from the hedgerow, torn
by the wind.

Emily and Marjorie noticed this.
Without saying why, they started to avoid the country way
through the cornfield. Instead they walked
from the farm up the road to the stop where they
caught the bus.

And it caught them. So in time they married.
Marjorie, divorced, rose high in the catering profession.
Emily had children and grandchildren, though,
with the farm sold, none found a cross to fit their clothes when
Emily and Marjorie died.

Leaving

Habits the hands have, reaching for this and that,
    (tea kettle, orange squeezer, milk jug,
    frying pan, sugar jar, coffee mug)
manipulate, or make, a habitat,
become its *genii loci*, working on
quietly in the kitchen when you've gone.

Objects a house keeps safe on hooks and shelves
    (climbing boots, garden tools, backpacks
    bird feeders, tennis balls, anoraks)
the day you leave them bleakly to themselves,
do they decide how long, behind the door,
to keep your personality in store?

Good Bishop Berkeley made the objects stay
just where we leave them when we go away
by lending them to God. If so, God's mind
is crammed with things abandoned by mankind
    (featherbeds, chamber pots, flint lighters,
    quill pens, sealing wax, typewriters),

an archive of the infinitely there.
But there for whom? For what museum? And where?
I like to think of spiders, moths, white worms
leading their natural lives in empty rooms
    (egg-sacks, mouse-litter, dead flies,
    cobwebs, silverfish, small eyes)

while my possessions cease to study me
    (*Emma, The Signet Shakespeare, Saving Whales.*
    Living with Mushrooms, Leviathan, Wild Wales).
Habit by habit, they sink through time to be
one with the mind or instinct of the place,
home in its shadowy silence and stone space.

On Going Deaf

I've lost a sense. Why should I care?
Searching myself, I find a spare.
I keep that sixth sense in repair
And set it deftly, like a snare.

To witness pain is a different form of pain

The worm in the spine,
the word on the tongue—
not the same.
We speak of 'pain'.
The sufferer won't suffer it
to be tamed.

There's a shyness, no,
a privacy,
a pride in us. Don't divide us
into best and lesser.

Some of us, 'brave'? 'clever'?
watch at the mouth of it.
A woman vanishes,
eyes full of it, into it,
the grey cave of pain;
an animal drills
unspeakable growth for cover.

Outside, we pace in guilt
Ah, 'guilt', another name.

Not to reproach
is tact she learns to suffer.
And not to relax her speechless
grip on power.

Postscriptum

Now I am dead,
no words,
just a wine
of my choosing.

Drink to my
mute consent,
my rite of
dissolving.

Over my chalk
eyelids and wax skin
let a wild
reticence in.

Not a tear
or false look.
Poems, stay there
in your book.

Should passion
attend me,
let it flow freely
through Messiaen's

End of Time Quartet:
unendurable riddles
for the clarinet,
resolved in a fiddle's

remorseless,
forgiving ascent.

A Report from the Border

Wars in peacetime don't behave like wars.
So loving they are.
Kissed on both cheeks, silk-lined ambassadors
Pose and confer.

Unbuckle your envy, drop it there by the door.
We will settle,
We will settle without blows or bullets
The unequal score.

In nature, havenots have to be many
And havelots few.
Making money out of making money
Helps us help you.

This from the party of good intent. From the other,
Hunger's stare,
Drowned crops, charred hopes, fear, stupor, prayer
And literature.

Haunted

It's not when you walk through my sleep
That I'm haunted most.
I am also alive where you were.
And my own ghost.

Hearing with My Fingers

A house with a six-foot rosewood piano, too grand
to get out the door? *You buy it, I'll play it!*
So now, as in my childhood, the living-room
has become the piano room, exercising,
like a sun, irresistible powers of gravitation.
How to walk past and not be dragged to keys
that free at a touch the souls of the composers?
The piano itself is soul-shaped. Like lovers,
our baby grands lay deep in each other's curves;
players locked eyes across the Yin and Yang of them,
fingering delight in a marriage of true sounds.

How would a living-room live without pianos,
I used to wonder, beginning my before-breakfast
two-hour stint at the Steinway—scales, arpeggios,
Czerny or cheery Scarlatti, progressing through Bach
(stirrings in the kitchen, waftings of coffee and bacon)
to *Scenes from Childhood* that my hands, to my head's
amazement, still remember after forty years' neglect.

If I fancied myself an object of fate's attention,
I'd take for punishment the fog blinding my ears.
What was I doing those waste, egotistical years
when I snatched what I heard and never told the piano?
I wanted a contract with love. I wanted the words!
And now, apparently, my fingers have forgiven me.
Wordless as right and left, as right and wrong,

drained of ambition, gullied with veiny skin,
they want to go back and teach my eyes to listen,
my heart to see . . . the shape of a Greek amphora,
plum-blossom after Hiroshima, harmony-seeds
growing from staves my clumsy fingers read.

A Marriage

When my mother knew why her treatment wasn't
    working,
She said to my father, trying not to detonate her news,
'Steve, you must marry again. When I'm gone, who's
    going
To tell you to put your trousers on before your shoes?'

My father opened his mouth to—couldn't—refuse.
Instead, he threw her a look; a man just shot
Gazing at the arm or leg he was about to lose.
His cigarette burned him, but he didn't stub it out.

Later, on the porch, alive in the dark together,
How solid the house must have felt, how sanely familiar
The night-lit leaves, their shadows patterning the street.
The house is still there. The elms and the people, not.

It was now, and it never was now. Like every experience
Of being entirely here, yet really not being.
They couldn't imagine the future that I am seeing,
For all his philosophy and all her common sense.

Washing My Hair

Contending against a restless shower-head,
     I lather my own.
The hot tap, without a mind, decides
     to scald me;
The cold, without a will, would rather
     freeze me.
Turning them to suit me is an act of flesh
     I know as mine.
Here I am: scalp, neck, back, breasts,
     armpits, spine,
Parts I've long been part of, never
     treasured much,
Since I absorb them not *by* touch, more
     because of touch.
It's my mind, with its hoard of horribles,
     that's me.
Or is it really? I fantasise it bodiless,
     set free:
No bones, no skin, no hair, no nerves,
     just memory,
Untouchable, unwashable, and not, I guess,
     my own.
Still, none will know me better when I'm
     words on stone
Than I, these creased familiar hands
     and clumsy feet.
My soul, how will I recognise you
     if we meet?

Who's Joking with the Photographer?

(*Photographs of myself approaching seventy*)

(*for Ernestine Ruben*)

Not my final face, a map of how to get there.
Seven ages, seven irreversible layers, each
subtler and more supple than a snake's skin.
Nobody looks surprised when we slough off one
and begin to inhabit another.
Do we exchange them whole in our sleep, or
are they washed away in pieces, cheek by brow by chin,
in the steady abrasions of the solar shower?
Draw first breath, and time turns on its taps.
No wonder the newborn's tiny face crinkles and cries:
chill, then a sharp collision with light,
the mouth's desperation for the foreign nipple,
all the uses of eyes, ears, hands still to be learned
before the self pulls away in its skin-tight sphere
to endure on its own the tectonic geology of childhood.

Imagine in space-time irretrievable mothers viewing
the pensioners their babies have become.
'Well, that's life, nothing we can do about it now.'
They don't love us as much as they did, and
why should they? We have replaced them. Just as we're
being replaced by big sassy kids in school blazers.
Meanwhile, Federal Express has delivered my sixth
    face—

grandmother's, scraps of me grafted to her bones.
I don't believe it. Who made this mess,
this developer's sprawl of roads that can't be retaken,
high tension wires that run dangerously under the skin?
What is it the sceptical eyes are saying to the twisted lips:
ambition is a cliché, beauty a banality? In any case,
this face has given them up—old friends whose
        obituaries
it reads in the mirror with scarcely a regret.

So, who's joking with the photographer?
And what did she think she was doing,
taking pictures of the impossible? Was a radioscope
attached to her lens? Something teasing under the skull
has infiltrated the surface, something you can't see
until you look away, then it shoots out and tickles you.
You could call it soul or spirit, but that would be serious.
Look for a word that mixes affection with insurrection,
frivolity, child's play, rude curiosity,
a willingness to lift the seventh veil and welcome Yorick.
That's partly what the photo says. The rest is private:
guilt that rouses memory at four in the morning,
truths such as Hamlet used, torturing his mother,
all the dark half-tones of the sensuous unsayable
finding a whole woman there, in her one face.

To Phoebe

(at five months)

How in this mindless whirl of time and space
Find words to welcome one small human child?
Shakespeare was lucky, art wore Shakespeare's face,
And nature kept the virtues neatly filed.
God's earth was fixed, and round it ran the sun,
A temperamental lantern on a skate.
Our lives by stars were wound up or begun;
The universe was Heaven's unspoiled estate.

But now, lost to the angels, it appears
We share with rats and fleas a murky source.
Our plaited genes mean nothing to the spheres;
Contingency, not prayer, will plot your course.

Yet no small Phoebe *circa* 1603
Was ever free to be what you shall be.

In the Weather of Deciduous Souls

Vermont, 2003

(for Jay Parini, and for Laura and Franklin Reeve)

Why don't you Vermonters call October
All Souls' Carnival? Dying and dyed,
The trees dress up in cerements, and here's your
Road show's kinky, country celebration,

Gold leaf and confetti every citybilly
Comes to gawp at, while the scenery collapses
And the lights come down in whooshes of wind
(There's the wind will blow the winter in)
Burying one more year in torn-off days—
Some ashy, some embers,
Some so flushed with going
You want to keep them warm, like happiness,
Like wine that can't be guzzled from the glass,
Like visits from love or sunsets,
Like riotous hours that won't grow stale, but last.
They want so much to be sewn back on the tree.
They want, like you and me, not to be past.

Stone Milk

Sils-Maria, Graubunden, 2006

A backward May, with all the local finches of the Fex Tal
        piping in dialect.
'Gruezi' to the nun-white finger-high crocuses
        thinly nursing to life the flattened fields.
'Gruezi' to the fisted bristles colouring the larches
        a green to break your heart.
The fairytale resorts, scrubbed clean but closed
        because the coach crowds haven't arrived yet,
look to be hospitals for convalescent ideals.

Imagine a breath held long before history happened,
allowing a lake to drown its Jurassic numbness
        in Elysian blue.

Conceive of the gentians' daytime midnight 'smoking
     torch-like out of Pluto's gloom',
Eden's anemones lifting from pale Blakean nightgowns
     faces of incorruptible innocence.
If stones could be milked, these fleeting rivers of melt
     would feed us like flowering trees,
since Mother Earth, you say, after eons of glacial
     childbirth
          brings up her whole brood naturally.

But naturally what I want and need and expect is to be
     loved.
So why, as I grow older, when I lift up my eyes to the
     hills—
          raw deserts that they are—
do they comfort me (not always but sometimes)
     with the pristine beauty of my almost absence?
Not the milk of kindness but the milk of stones
     is food I'm learning to long for.

Before Eden

(*for Paul Stangroom*)

A day opens, a day closes,
Each day like every other day.
No day is like another day.

A wave crashes, a wave caresses,
Each wave like the next wave.
None sweeps the same arc on the sand.

A wall fits its belt to a hill
As a mason fits stone to hand.
No stone's like any other stone,

And every stone has a like stone.
Why should another spring surprise me?
The gorse still erupts from the scrubland,

The gulls again screech to the landfill.
What claims identity
That isn't self-propelled, vicious, multiple, alone?

Think of how it was before Eden.
God held his breath,
The fresh-moulded clay in his hands,

Hesitating between dream and achievement.
The mountains were there,
Fixed in a clear, viscous element

He would need to exchange for air.
Trees flowered, gorgeous as palaces,
All without fruit, without rot.

Had bacteria and seeds been invented?
Yes, but they didn't have uses.
The birds and creatures were there,

Evolved already in his mind,
Lifelessly waiting while
The pivotal question tormented him:

What sort of nature did he want?
Once he'd breathed life into Adam,
He knew he couldn't take it back!

He himself might have to be
Re-created, risking
His hand-crafted system, risking death.

No life without birth.
No growth without waste.
No first step without a last.

It was such perfect weather,
That sparkling morning of the sixth day
When God, in his pride, looked over

His hard week's work, saw that it was good.
And hesitated.
If the sky had admitted one cloud,

If the mountains had understood
The whispering ice
Or loved the molten nature of being,

If a bird had cried out, or if
A locust had filleted sound,
Or if terror had *said* . . .

He might have thought the fifth day would suffice.
But the *Gipfeln* nursing the rhododendrons,
Even the Tree of Knowledge, said nothing.

It was silence that broke him in the end.
With every perfect day identical,
No animating evil could arise.

So God bent down and sighed the words,
'I will.'
He spoke, and Adam opened all his eyes.

The Enigma

Falling to sleep last night in a deep crevasse
between one rough dream and another, I seemed,
still awake, to be stranded on a stony path,
and there the familiar enigma presented itself
in the shape of a little trembling lamb.
It was lying like a pearl in the trough between
one Welsh slab and another, and it was crying.

I looked around, as anyone would, for its mother.
Nothing was there. What did I know about lambs?
Should I pick it up? Carry it . . . where?
What would I do if it were dying? The hand
of my conscience fought with the claw of my fear.
It wasn't so easy to imitate the Good Shepherd
in that faded, framed Sunday School picture
filtering now through the dream's daguerreotype.

With the wind fallen and the moon swollen to the full,
small, white doubles of the creature at my feet
flared like candles in the creases of the night
until it looked to be alive with new born lambs.
Where could they all have come from?
A second look, and the bleating lambs were birds—
kittiwakes nesting, clustered on a cliff face,
fixing on me their dark accusing eyes.

There was a kind of imperative not to touch them,
yet to be of them, whatever they were—
now lambs, now birds, now floating points of light—
fireflies signalling how many lost New England
    summers?
One form, now another; one configuration, now
    another.
Like fossils locked deep in the folds of my brain,
outliving a time by telling its story. Like stars.

Orcop

Remembering Frances Horovitz (1938–1983)

Driving south from Hereford one day in March
memorable for trickling piles of snow, with sideshows,
drift upon drift of snowdrops lapping the hedgerows,
we sighted the signpost, and on impulse, turned up
the winding, vertical road to Orcop. The church,
further away from the village than I remembered,
was no less an image of you than I remembered,

with its high-pitched, peasant roof and wooden steeple
gracing a slope with yew trees and a painter's view—
ploughed red soil, a pasture, a working barn—
that set it apart from the ordinary, just as your field stone,
when we found it, set you apart from the good people
labelled in polished marble, buried around you.
As in your life, though never aloof, you were alone.
I remembered how, when you quietly entered a room
in one of those woven dresses you used to wear,
heather or lavender, all senseless chattering would cease,
shamed by your dignity. I remembered your beautiful
    things:
your pots, your books, your cat, silver as your cross,
your delicate drawings. Yes, I remembered you exactly.
And there you were, still—beautiful, exceptional,
in a landscape of lichen I had to read like Braille
to find your name. I heard the first blackbird, then a
    thrush.
Later, as we left, the children we'd seen playing
among the graves when we arrived resumed their game,
using your stone, a hump from another century,
to hide behind, while one, the smallest, counted slowly.

Inheriting My Grandmother's Nightmare

Consider the adhesiveness of things
    to the ghosts that prized them,
the 'olden days' of birthday spoons
    and silver napkin rings.

Too carelessly I opened
    that velvet drawer of heirlooms.
There lay my grandmother's soul
begging under veils of tarnish to be brought back whole.

She who was always a climate in herself,
    who refused to vanish
as the nineteen-hundreds grew older and louder
    and the wars worse
and her grandchildren, bigger and ruder
    in her daughter's house.
How completely turned around
her lavender world became, how upside down.

And how much, under her 'flyaway' hair,
    she must have suffered,
sitting there ignored by the dinner guests
    hour after candle-lit hour,
rubbed out, like her initials on the silverware,
    eating little, passing bread,
until the wine's flood, the smoke's blast,
the thunderous guffaws at last roared her to bed.

In her tiny garden of confidence,
    wasted she felt, and furious.
She fled to church, but Baby Jesus
    had outgrown his manger.
She read of Jews in *The New Haven Register*
    gassed or buried alive.
Every night, at the wheel of an ambulance,
she drove and drove, not knowing how to drive.

She died in '55, paralysed, helpless.
    Her no-man's-land survived.
I light my own age with a spill
    from her distress. And there it is,
her dream, my heirloom, my drive downhill
    at the wheel of the last bus,
the siren's wail, the smoke, the sickly smell.
The drawer won't shut again. It never will.

Beach Kites

Is this a new way of being born?
To feel some huge crescent personality
burgeoning out of your shoulders,
winging you over the sand, the sluggish sea?
Mile upon mile of contaminated Wash is
tucking a cold March sky into the horizon.

You can drive no further.
Look down at the thrashing water,
the upfalls of its reach
failing, failing again to take the cliff—
sandpipers hunch on the geomorphic ledge—
rock face and wave force, story without speech.

But it's one thing to pause at the cutting edge,
another to face the evolving beach, the gap
where the road stops and the dunes heap
and the wind blows fiercely in the wrong direction.

One gaudy comma ascends . . . another . . .
　　　another . . .
the air is rocking alert with punctuation.

Grey sickle cells cluster under a microscope.

A jumbo wasp, a pterodactyl, a peacock feather
jockey for space against moon-parings, rainbow
　　　zeppelins,
prayer flags—imagination battling with imagination,
spotted species chasing the plain—as out they float,
strong men steering their wild umbilical toys

away from the girlfriends in the car park, who
leathered from heel to neck in steel-studded black,
headscarfed against the wind, seem coolly resigned
to an old dispensation, a ritual of mating
that puts up again with the cliff-hanging habits of boys.
Is this a new way of writing?
The heroes off flying or fighting, the women waiting?

Variations on a Line by Peter Redgrove

(*for Penelope Shuttle, remembering Evangeline Paterson*)

'A wind blows through the clock.'
Washes its spinning mesh of brass
with the same salt
that files down whorls in the whelk's shell,
slipper shell and spindle shell.

It's wind whistling through the clock
that licks away the blue plastic eyes
of the lost doll clotted with slime,
that also shapes jewels
made of ruby bright bottle glass
and heavy footballs of mortar-crossed brick.
The beach is smoothed to simplicity
by repeated beatings, and by a silicon tick

through which the wind blows,
bowling its weight along the shore
where waves of surf report on waves of shale,
a lacy froth of unresolved dispute
between the tides of water and the tides of rock.

A spider's curtain flutters
from bric-à-brac inside a sheep's skull
scrubbed with sand. What's more persistent
than a spider in a sheep's skull? A woman, knitting,
taking refuge from the wars of the beach
in a pleasant parlour, a perfectly-regulated clock.

Listen to the wind blowing through her,
through her knitting, through her poems
scrubbed of anxiety. Think of her saying quietly,
'I know what he means, it's comfort to me,
the everlasting breath of God I hear
sweeping through the clock.'

Think of the breath that's been trapped
in the clock, locked up in coal seams,
imprisoned in deep pockets hacked from rock
under slate black weather in slate black Wales.

Or maybe the wind is the voice of the clock
wailing to cohorts of lichened stone
built to hold fast the tribal hills,
telling tales, telling tales through the wind's mouth
that has blown out those makers like candles.

Think of the breath of the English poets
funnelled through England's Pleistocene fells,
scribbling in foam on the Lakes.
How long can a line last
that is writ on water? Or with ink on paper?
Or with fingertips on computer?
Compare it to the writing of ice on rock,
to the sea erasing millimetre by millimetre
mud books and fossil prints
from tall crumbling shelves along the shore.

Think of the spirits blowing through the clock,
shouting, 'death shall have no dominion,'
as death swirls them out, delighted, on the tide.
Think of the sillion shine of Hopkins' mind,
of Wordsworth's mortal immortality,
its clock still ticking, its bell
still tolling, as the years tumble over him,
not asleep between births,
but waking when the world's breath blows through him.

And singing, as your ashes were singing, Peter,
in September, on Maenporth Beach,
as the waves swirled them out in rhythm with the tide,
and the wind told the clock to greet them.

CORRESPONDENCES

A Family History in Letters

To Philip Hobsbaum,
and in memory of my mother,
Louise Destler Stevenson

CHRONOLOGY

INTRODUCTION: THE FAMILY

Genealogy: The Chandler Family   *108*

1968   An Obituary: Mrs Neil F. Arbeiter   *109*

1968   Eden Ann Whitelaw to her sister Kay
Boyd in London   *110*

1968   From *The Clearfield Enquirer*: Clearfield's
New Public Monument and Museum   *115*

PART ONE: IN THE HAND OF THE LORD, 1829–1929

1829   Condolences of a minister to his bereaved
daughter after the death of her young
husband in a shipwreck off Halifax, N.S.   *118*

1830   The Minister's wife, in confidence, to a
beloved sister during a January storm   *121*

1830   *An Obituary:* The Minister's Wife   *123*

1832   A prodigal son: Reuben Chandler is
stricken with guilt in New Orleans, having
run away from restricting regimes at home
and at Harvard College   *123*

1838   A family blunder: Elizabeth Chandler
Boyd writes to her brother Reuben on
the occasion of his engagement to a
Southerner   *129*

1840   A daughter's difficulties as a wife: Mrs
Reuben Chandler to her mother in
New Orleans   *132*

1849   Fragments: Mrs Reuben Chandler writes
to her husband during a cholera epidemic   *137*

1855   A blunder rectified: A final word from
        Cincinnati businessman, Reuben Chandler,
        to his runaway wife   *139*

1859   A successful American advises his sons
        studying abroad: Reuben Chandler to his
        sons in Geneva   *140*

1864   Letter to a mother from a Confederate
        soldier: Matthew Chandler to Marianne
        Lavalle Chandler   *142*

1867   Notes to a father from a young man gone
        west: Jacob Chandler to his father Reuben
        Chandler   *143*

1895   Maxims of a Christian businessman:
        From the journal of Jacob M. Chandler,
        Cincinnati's Citizen of the Year   *146*

1896   A worried father writes to his daughter at
        Oberlin College: Jacob Chandler to his
        daughter Maura   *148*

1900   A New Year's Message to myself:
        From the journal of Maura Chandler
        on the eve of her marriage to Ethan
        Amos Boyd   *151*

1910   A vigorous letter from a salesman of the
        Lord: Ethan Amos Boyd to his wife
        Maura   *154*

1929   From *The Clearfield Enquirer*: A Notice of
        Insolvency   *156*

1929   A letter to God on hotel notepaper from
        Ethan Amos Boyd   *156*

PART TWO: WOMEN IN MARRIAGE, 1930–1968

1968   A London letter: The poet, Kay Boyd,
       replies ambiguously to her sister in
       Clearfield   *158*

1930   Two Cambridges: A letter from Maura
       Chandler Boyd to her daughter Ruth
       Arbeiter in England   *160*

1936   A letter from an English novelist: Paul
       Maxwell, author of *A Second Eve*,
       writes to Ruth Arbeiter in Vermont   *163*

1936   Two Poems and a Rejection Slip: From
       the notebooks of Ruth Arbeiter   *166*

1945   A Love Letter: Ruth Arbeiter to Major
       Paul Maxwell   *168*

1954   From an Asylum: Kathy Chattle to her
       mother, Ruth Arbeiter   *170*

1954   Mrs Lillian Culick, divorcée, to Dr
       Frank Chattle   *177*

1968   End of a summer's day: From the journal
       of Ruth Arbeiter   *181*

PART THREE: LIVING FOR NOW

1968   Professor Arbeiter to his dead wife   *185*

1968   Nick Arbeiter writes poems on the road
       to Wyoming after a funeral in Vermont   *187*

1972   Epilogue: Kay Boyd to her father,
       Professor Arbeiter   *194*

GENEALOGY
*The Chandler Family**

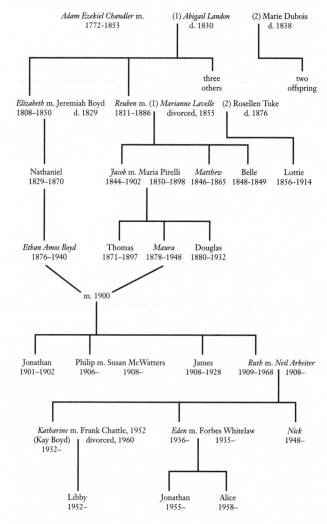

Adam Ezekiel Chandler m. (1) *Abigail Landon*   (2) Marie Dubois
1772–1853   d. 1830   d. 1838

three others   two offspring

Elizabeth m. Jeremiah Boyd   *Reuben* m. (1) *Marianne Lavelle*   (2) Rosellen Tuke
1808–1850   d. 1829   1811–1886   divorced, 1855   d. 1876

Nathaniel
1829–1870

Jacob m. Maria Pirelli   *Matthew*   Belle   Lottie
1844–1902   1850–1898   1846–1865   1848–1849   1856–1914

Ethan Amos Boyd
1876–1940

Thomas   *Maura*   Douglas
1871–1897   1878–1948   1880–1932

m. 1900

Jonathan   Philip m. Susan McWatters   James   *Ruth* m. *Neil Arbeiter*
1901–1902   1906–   1908–   1908–1928   1909–1968   1908–

Katharine m. Frank Chattle, 1952   *Eden* m. Forbes Whitelaw   *Nick*
(Kay Boyd)   divorced, 1960   1936–   1935–   1948–
1932–

Libby
1952–

Jonathan   Alice
1955–   1958–

*The names in italic are represented by letters in this book

THE CLEARFIELD ENQUIRER

JULY 5, 1968

Obituary

On the 4th of July, Mrs Neil F. Arbeiter, née Ruth Chandler Boyd, died peacefully in the Vermont State Hospital in Bennington. Mrs Arbeiter was a descendant of the Chandler family whose history is intimately connected with the town of Clearfield. She was fifty-nine years of age.

Mrs Arbeiter was the only daughter of the lay preacher and social reformer, Ethan Amos Boyd. She was born in Clearfield in 1909, when the Chandler House was the center of an experiment in Community and Christian Living conducted by her father. From 1926 until 1930 she attended Oberlin College in Ohio where she graduated *Phi Beta Kappa*, *Magna Cum Laude*. She was married in 1930 to Neil Freisingham Arbeiter, the Harvard historian, and is survived by him and her three children: Mrs Katharine Ann Chattle, now domiciled in London, England, Mrs Eden Whitelaw of Clearfield, and an only son, Nicholas, who is about to enter his Senior year at Dartmouth College in New Hampshire.

During the painful years preceding her death, Mrs Arbeiter courageously persevered in those works for the public welfare which distinguished her all her life as a New Englander and a patriot. A founding member of the Halifax County League of Women Voters, she was three times elected to the State Board. She was an active supporter of Planned Parenthood, a member of the State Committee for the Preservation of Wild Life, and the author of four pamphlets in the *This is your United Nations* series.

She will be lovingly remembered for her selfless dedication to her country, to her church, to her family and friends. Funeral services will be conducted in the First Presbyterian Church tomorrow, July 6th, at 4.15 p.m. The family requests that no flowers be sent but that donations be made instead to the American Cancer Society.

Eden Ann Whitelaw to her sister Kay Boyd in London

NOVEMBER 5, 1968   **MOSSY HOUSE,**
                              CLEARFIELD, VERMONT

Dear Kay. So . . . a summer.
    Four months since she died.
        And your decision not to return,
wise, I wonder?
        Because of course you're missed.
            Poor father!
He's in no mood for anger.
    Tries to live normally:
        office hours, meals, long walks.
Sundays, his string quartet.

You know what's become of the house.
    He asked me to clear it.
        Mother's desk, books, correspondences,

piles of old stuff, mostly letters.
    'Too busy' his excuse.
        Meaning that the dear couldn't face it,
the uselessness, pain of a return
    to a place she's still alive in.
For if she's a ghost, she's here,
        is this house.

Now every day I'm like my own ghost
    moving within hers.
      I blow off the usual mouse droppings
        (packing the stoneware).
I swat late wasps.
    I air out the stale rugs, blankets.
      Then sit up nights.
In the silence.
    The children are asleep
      upstairs in our childstained bedrooms.

Only I in her room,
    her blue wall paper.
      It ought to keep her out!
It ought to keep her dead to what it's come to!
    A stump with its root in her grave.
      An Amen to us.

Yes, and I'd like to save everything,
    have it again.
      Our summers for our children.

Picnicking, haying, those
   purple-mouthed banquets after berry-picking,
      dawdling days, naked in the brook;
or just the naming of places:
   The Star Rock, The Bear Pits, The Druids,
      the view from the hill.

It all seemed interminable in those days.

And now I'm over thirty,
   looking back, looking on.
      Hunched on the spindly pink sofa under the
         lithographs,
reading and sorting, rereading . . .
   dead evidences, grievances, a
      yellowing litter of scraps scratched over with lives.

So I cry and cry and then
   wish there were some way to justify
      the release of it.
For it's not for her particular death,
   but for what dies with her.
                  Something that calls
for our abduction
   out of things. Nostalgia
      for expended generations.

Yet never more lovely,
   this North-East, this November.
      Maples, barren as wires . . . like

seas of spun wire
between the swell of the cloudbanks
and the black shelving continents of pine.
The hills turn silver in the sun,
a kind of necessary silver,
until the seasons converge there,
meeting in confusion,
the blown leaves and snowflakes
fountaining together.

Then night after night
I dream the same nightmare.
On the last warm day
We all go down to the lake.
We all drive down to the beach
at the edge of the lake.
But the lake's shrunk away from its lips
and lies small as a river,
and the beach is the lake's wrecked floor,
wrack and litter.
And the children,
they tear off their shoes,
steal ahead of us, beachcombing.
We adults stalk behind,
parents,
two of us, loitering.

And the sky is very blue
and the slick mud, silver, and the
bare posts are like nails

pulled up out of their shadows.
      Oh, you'd say summer,
              but the woods are grey.
Then a jeep jolts down to the quay
      and two men get out. They
          shuffle a flat-bottomed boat
to the edge of the water,
      climb in and pull themselves, float by
         float by float along a rope
lying slack on the harbor.
      We watch them reel it in,
doubled, always, by water.

And then the children,
      who have rounded the shore,
         cluster opposite, jeering.

Their arms are full of driftwood,
      and their faces so clear
         we seem to share them with some
menace or fascination
      as the boat crawls nearer.
      Then I know they will be gone.
I never will be able to retrieve them.
      I cry out.
      Stumble forward.

Come back! Come back!
      They seem not to hear.
      And then the children are not our children,

but us.

    Not Jonathan, Libby, Alice, but
        you, me, Nicholas.

That's when I wake,
    usually as now, with the dawn
        grey and cold in the empty window.

Kay, please come home.
    Please won't you come home?
        Come help me keep her alive a little longer.

THE CLEARFIELD ENQUIRER

NOVEMBER 8, 1968

Clearfield's New Public Monument and Museum

An Historical Note on the Chandler Home

According to Mrs Eden Whitelaw, a daughter of the late Mrs Neil F. Arbeiter who died last July, the Chandler Home is to be opened to the public next summer. Professor Arbeiter has agreed to its being used as a museum and library, and Mrs Whitelaw, who will continue to reside with her family in 'The Old Red Barn' next door, assures us that the original furniture will be preserved, and that a selection of family letters will be made available to the public.

The Chandler family was established in New England when Reverend Adam Ezekiel Chandler emigrated from Yorkshire in 1789. In 1807 he married a daughter of the Landon family in New Haven, after which he settled in what was then called 'Mossy House' in Clearfield. Until his death in 1853 he preached Hell-fire and abolition from the pulpit of the First Presbyterian Church. He was famous throughout New England for his uncompromising Calvinism and for his devotion to the cause of Negro emancipation in the South.

During the 1830s and 40s, the Chandler home was a station in the 'underground railway' which aided escaped slaves to flee north into Canada. After the Civil War, the house passed into an era of austere elegance under the ownership of Dr Chandler's grandson, the wealthy and pious Jacob M. Chandler of Chandler Stores, Inc., Cincinnati and Boston. In 1902 the property descended to Jacob's daughter, Maura, who had married the social reformer, Ethan A. Boyd in 1900. Boyd converted the house into a dormitory and retreat for city factory workers. In 1909 it became the center of an experiment in cooperative socialist living, the 'Eden' of English novelist Paul W. Maxwell's *A Second Eve*. In 1929 Ethan Boyd went bankrupt. He ended his days in 1940, a broken and tragic figure, in a mental institution in New York State.

Despite the Great Depression, the Cincinnati Insurance magnate, Herman Arbeiter, was able to save the Chandler estate when his son, Neil, married Ethan and Maura Boyd's only daughter, Ruth, in 1930. The house has passed on through the Arbeiters to the descendants of the original Chandlers who have generously made provision for their home to be a community monument.

There is no doubt that the Chandler Home remains today a link with our town's great past. We hope it will stand as a monument to Yankee common sense and idealism at this time when the oldest American institutions are in jeopardy. In the teeth of subversion and doubt, let us keep one corner of our dear New England bright and unspoiled. Let us honor our traditions and the dedicated spirit of our ancestors—honest, hard-working, decent Christian Americans—for the sake of whom and whose children Ruth Arbeiter did not live and die in vain.

PART ONE
In the Hand of the Lord
1829–1929

Letters and documents selected from the Chandler Family
Archives of the Chandler Memorial Library, Clearfield, Ver-
mont . . . being a partial record of members of the family
descended from Adam Ezekiel Chandler who was from 1807
until his death in 1853 Minister of the First Presbyterian
Church of Clearfield, in the County of Halifax.

*Condolences of a minister to his bereaved daughter
after the death of her young husband in a
shipwreck off Halifax, N.S.*

SEPTEMBER 3, 1829   **CLEARFIELD, VERMONT**

My wretched daughter,

I have studied your letter with exacting and impartial
        attention.
What shall I say?
Except that I suffer, as you, too, must suffer
increasingly from a sense of the justice of your
        bereavement.

What did you expect, Elizabeth,
from your childhood preferring, despite my
        prognostications,
the precarious apartments of the world
to the safer premises of the spirit.

Have I not heard you declare, and on more than one
      occasion,
that only if your earthly aspirations should be cut down
would you cast yourself upon the Mercy of God?

What your conduct has been your conscience will teach
      you.
What God in his Justice has performed is plain enough.

Is is possible you imagine you have claims on his Infinite
      Mercy?
Even presupposing that God has summoned you this
      sacrifice,
do you deem it in the interest of The Lord to secure
      your favor?
Is not sacrifice punishment of Sin?
Is it not through God's Will that we all do not perish
instantly? Instantaneously consumed!

Avoid, my child, those rocks on which multitudes have
      been wrecked!
Think not to gain peace with The Lord by measuring
Immutable Requirements with the petty inch rule of
      ability!
His requirements of you are but three:
Repentance. Faith. Love. Only these.
How often in my life has some Act of the Almighty
opened vast caverns of tempestuous night and
      vicissitude!
Yet never before have I felt so keenly, so intimately,
the power of His Unfathomable Choice.

Such a talent cut off!
Scholarship. Humility. Devotion to
Truth and Duty. All in a twinkling rendered useless by
  that
Hand of Mysterious Providence which plunges like
  lightning
into the heart of us, scooping, as it were,
but a single drop from the tainted well, swelling,
could we but see it, with the waters of human iniquity
the Eternal River of Heaven which flows from the
  Throne!

How can I give you the comfort you desire?
Turn rather to that Shepherd you have rejected.
Let him bear you to His Glorious Pastures
where in company with the Chosen of His Flock
you may content your soul with the reflection that
what is loss to you is gain immeasurable to that
dear one now with God.
                    For
fine as was his spirit upon this earth,
drawn down by the body which confined it—
what now must it be, washed white in the Blood of the
  Lamb,
drenched daily in that Inexhaustible Spring
which is the source of our Everlasting Joy?

My blessing upon you and upon your little one.
May you find in the Love of Jesus hope you had
    abandoned.
May the Light of His Countenance shine upon you and
give you peace, now and in the Life Everlasting.

From your loving father on earth who lives in
The Lord,

Adam Chandler

*The Minister's wife, in confidence, to a beloved sister
during a January storm*

JANUARY 14, 1830   **CLEARFIELD, VERMONT**

My dear Eliza,

Your letter came to hand in good time.
Would answer it at length were it not
for vexations: weather like the Arctic,
violent storms, no wood cut. Dr Chandler
gone to Boston. Youth from Harvard
in exchange here, sprawled by the one fire,
bawling for malmsey, concocting us morsels
for tomorrow's theological banquet while we
shiver on his polar side, hungry for the supper
our wet coals smoke but won't cook!

Anne's in bed. Grippe. And Elizabeth
frantic lest her Nathan, who has weak lungs,
contract it. Black Beck's in the pantry.
I can hear her, poor woman, screaming through
four closed doors. A finger. She crushed it
in the clothes mangle. Doubt she'll save it.

So, with one thing and another,
my reading flags. I average, perhaps,
a page a week. Must content myself,
I fancy, with the learning I possess, or
glean what I can from the backs of newspapers.
I've learned this: Alkalis are thought to be
metal oxides. How I rejoice in this fact.

But the children all ail, and not noiselessly.
Each day's a struggle. Scant food. Stacked drifts.
The horses, sheep, sickly, and poor Bob,
the Labrador, dead in the hayloft, forgotten
after last week's rat-catching!
Alas, I must stop.
My hand's gone numb.
The stove's gone out.
I pray you,
        keep well and God bless you.

                From your everloving sister,

                        Abigail Chandler

NEW ENGLAND
PRESBYTERIAN GAZETTE

SEPTEMBER 6, 1830

Obituary
The Minister's Wife

On September 3rd, in the thirty-ninth year of her life in the Lord, Mrs Abigail Landon Chandler, dearly beloved wife of our pastor and brother in Christ, Reverend Dr Adam E. Chandler of the First Presbyterian Church of Clearfield in the County of Halifax, Vermont. She leaves desolate a husband and five children.

In the time of earthly sorrows let us remember that for this pious woman Death was not a termination but a transition.

In its infinite peace, her soul is even now amongst us.

A prodigal son: Reuben Chandler is stricken with guilt in New Orleans, having run away from restricting regimes at home and at Harvard College

JUNE 23, 1832   **NEW ORLEANS**

My dear father,
    That I write, sick,
        from a convent in New Orleans

may distress you less
    than that I write at all.
        Pray for my soul.

No.

      Satan has not tempted me with Popery.
          Likewise I turn from the Anti-Christ, Reason,
          with revulsion.

Yet I have been ill,
      disturbed in my mind,
          found unconscious on the road

by some pupils from this convent,
      struck down, nearly blind,
          from the power of a sun which,

to those bred in our blue Yankee climate,
      is a weapon of fire
          in the hand of the Adversary.

Yet I do not attribute my state
      to the heat or to illness.
          A dream has troubled me night after

night in this place.
      A vision so vivid,
          so beyond my powers of exorcism,

that I lay it in repentance at your feet.
      I regret my past wilfulness and wickedness.
          I beg you regard me as your son.

I dream I am walking on one of these
      high southern levees,
          a baked and dusty road,

pitted with human footprints,
    scarred deeply with cart tracks,
        and also with the tracks of cattle,

horses and sheep and other animals.
    This road I follow with my eyes, head
        lowered, afraid to look up or to the

right or left, though I feel,
    like a palpitating veil,
        the thick vegetation of the Bayou

looming from its moss;
    the fierce, silent pulse of the
        Mississippi; and the sun,

close above me,
    burning through its perishable,
        imagined membrane,

burning, enlarging,
    descending until I needs must,
        from the pressure of it,

kneel down forcibly in the dust,
    raising my hands to God for
        succor and mercy.

I look up.
    And lo, the dome of the Heavens
        is filled with the sun,

and its circle of horizon
is lashed with the sun's fiery tongues.

To my left,
an unbounded ocean
breathes in and exhales.

To my right,
not a jungle
but a desert!

Then I look upon the ocean
and see that it is made not of water
but of human bodies, hideous and naked;

men, women and children are being
swept up and dashed down,
yea, again and again and again

into vast eddies of one another.
And I see these are living beings,
some of our country and county.

There is Mad Mistress Beaton,
shorn of her rags, wig and spectacles.
And poor, harmless postmaster Brown,

hollow, like a sheep's skull,
but grey and elongated
like a tangle of weatherbeaten driftwood.

Always I seem to see my sister Elizabeth,
    but when I cry out, she
        throws back black strands of turbulently

heaving hair and stares horribly through me.
    The next morning she is flung from my sight
        and where she was . . . is now a coal black

negro, streaked with his blood,
    writhing and shaking his fists and wailing
        even as he vanishes,

'Follow me,
    and I will make you fishers of men!'

I turn then, in terror,
    to my right . . . to the desert
        where it spills out in miles and miles of

nothing at all.
    And I pray, as Christ prayed,
        for salvation through rejection of Evil.

And then I'm running
    mad with unquenchable thirst,
        between boulders and craters and

dry mountains, starved of vegetation.
    And then I am falling,
        and I fall

thus to wake in the sweat of my sheets,
    weeping like a child,
        stared at by some puzzled black-coiffed

hag who, roused from her sleep and
    doubtful of my sanity, stands beside me,
        uncertain of what to do.

What I am to think, father?
    What is Our Heavenly Father if
        such dreams are of his making?

What is His Love? His Omnipotence?
    His Challenge? His Forgiveness?
        Even His Retribution?

Meaningless as the flesh of that ocean?
    As the stones in that desert of sand?
        Does God, mocking, squat in detachment

behind a great mangle of sun,
    prescribing to the saved as to the damned,
        my own Hell on earth?

My pain . . . the ache of existence?

I remain your undeserving and most unhappy son,

Reuben Chandler

*A family blunder: Elizabeth Chandler Boyd writes
to her brother Reuben on the occasion of his
engagement to a Southerner*

SEPTEMBER 25, 1838　　　　　　**CLEARFIELD, VERMONT**

In truth, beloved brother,
　　　this news of your 'heart's arrangement'
　　　　　martyrs the best affections of my own.

Engaged!
　　　And to a Southerner!
　　　　　And how, pray, tell father?

If only you could see him . . . all but
　　　nailed to *The Emancipator*,
　　　　　racked by the Judas-justice of this land!

Four of our 'midnight Quakers'
　　　passed amongst us in a month
　　　　　and with precious, brave Marie so near her time,

the burden, as usual,
　　　devolved absolutely on me!
　　　　　I suppose there must be some good Southerners.

Well, Nathan and I are as
　　　calm as can be expected.
　　　　　I had (with reference to marriage)

put aside all mementoes of mine.
    I had thought the hurt healed
        and the scar strong.

But now the utter carelessness
    of your happiness (and selfishness)
        breaks through my aching wound like a
        vengeful worm!

Lost, lost, dearest friend!
    All his tokens I cherish
        (corpses in my little gilt box),

his ring,
    his portrait,
        the fine, silken flame of his hair . . .

they rise from the dead to me now
    like neglected ghosts
        and publish my blame from their shrine.

It happened one day
    as I sat (in tears) with his likeness,
        dear Nathaniel crept up to my knee.

'Who is this?' I asked smiling,
    (he saw I was weeping).
        'God,' he (so innocent) replied.

'My dear!' I reproved him.
    'Christ, then.'
        'No, *Papa*.'

'Yes, Papa, the same,' the child cried.
  'Is not Papa my Father,
    And Father is God,

And God changed to Jesus
  who died!'
    Just imagine my feelings!

I took him in my lap
  in a thunder-shower of kisses,
    saying 'Papa is *with* Jesus

because Jesus died *for* Papa.
  But we all will be with Papa
    when we die.'

And he cried . . . and even father—
  in a little while he joined us—
    cried, imploring us to pray!

And so we prayed
  and as we did, I felt
    a sunbeam spread about me

bearing in tender armfuls
  wondrous hope.
    And I saw my beloved husband

at rest in the bosom of Eternity,
  and my own soul, like your own,
    asleep on the Breast of the Lord.

So, now, my dear brother,
    may His light shine upon you,
        and give you His Peace and His Wisdom even
        now.

And may you be forgiven
    for the pain you have brought to others,

    from your loving and Christian sister,

    Elizabeth B

A daughter's difficulties as a wife: Mrs Reuben Chandler to her mother in New Orleans

SEPTEMBER 3, 1840   **CINCINNATI, OHIO**

Now that I've been married for almost four weeks, Mama,
    I'd better drop you and Papa dear a line.
        I guess I'm fine.

Ruby has promised to take me to the Lexington
    buggy races Tuesday, if the weather cools.
        So far we've not been out much.

Just stayed here stifling in hot Cincinnati.
    Clothes almost melt me, Mama, so I've not got out
        my lovely red velvet-and-silk pelisse yet,

or that sweet little lambskin coat with the fur hood.
  The sheets look elegant!
    I adore the pink monogram on the turnover

with exactly the same pattern on the pillowcases!
  Darlings!
    How I wish you could breeze in and admire
      them!

And the table linen,
  and the bone china,
    and the grand silver candlesticks,

and especially those
  long-stemmed Venetian wine glasses
    with the silver rims.

My, didn't your little daughter
  play the queen the other day
    serving dinner to a whole bevy of bachelors!

To tell the truth, Mama,
  Reuben was a silly to ask them,
    just imagine me, tiny wee me,

hostess to fourteen dragons
  and famished monsters,
    doing battle with fuming pipes and flying plugs.

Poor Rube!
  He doesn't chew and hardly ever smokes.
    He must have felt out of place.

I was frantic, naturally,
      for fear of wine stains and
            tobacco juice on the table cloth,

so I set Agatha to dart in and dab with a towel,
      and told Sue in the kitchen, to brew up some coffee
            quick, before they began speechmaking.

But it was no use.
      They would put me up on a chair after the ices,
            and one of them—Big Tom they call him—

(runs a sizable drygoods business here)
      well, this Tom pulled off my shoe,
            tried to drink wine out of it while

I was dying of laughter,
      and Tom was laughing too, when suddenly
            I slipped, and fell on the Flemish decanter!

It broke.
      Such a terrible pity.
            And so funny at the same time.

I must admit the boys were bricks,
      carrying the tablecloth out to the kitchen,
            holding it out while I

poured hot water from a height,
      just as you always said to.
            Everything would have been all right.

The party could have gone on.
    Then Reuben had to nose in and spoil things,
        sending me to bed!

So the boys went off, kind of sheepish.

Later Reuben said I had disgraced us
    and where was I brought up anyway,
        to behave like a bar maid!

But it wasn't my fault, Mama,
    They were his friends. He invited them.
        I like to give men a good time!

I'm writing this in bed because
    my head thumps and drums every time I move
        and I'm so dog tired!

The only time I sleep is in the morning
    when Reuben has left for the office.
        Which brings up a delicate subject, Mama.

I've been thinking and thinking,
    wondering whether I'll ever succeed in being
        the tender, devoted little wife you wanted me
            to be.

Because . . . oh, Mama,
    why didn't you tell me or warn me before I was
            married
        that a wife is expected to do it every night!

But how could we have guessed?
    Ruby came courting so cool and fine and polite,
        while beneath that gentlemanly, educated
            exterior . . .

well! I don't like to worry you, Mama.
    You know what men are like!
        I remember you said once the dears couldn't
        help it.

I try to be brave.
    But if you did have a chance to speak to Papa,
        mightn't you ask him to slip a word,

sort of man to man to Reuben . . .
    about how delicate I am
    and how sick I am every month,

not one of those cows
    who can be used and used!
        Someone's at the door.

I forgot,
    I asked Fanny Daniels to come up this morning
    to help fix a trim for my hat.

I'll have to hustle!
    Give all my love to dear Spooky and Cookie.
    How I miss them, the doggy darlings!

Oceans of hugs and kisses for you, too,
    and for precious Papa,

From your suffering and loving daughter,

Marianne

Fragments: Mrs Reuben Chandler writes to her husband during a cholera epidemic

NOTE: *Most of this journal, written on shipboard, seems to have been destroyed, probably by fire. What remains suggests that Mrs Chandler journeyed to New Orleans without her husband's permission, thus becoming indirectly the cause of her baby's death.*

AUGUST, 1849

EN ROUTE FROM NEW YORK TO NEW ORLEANS ABOARD THE 'GENERAL WAYNE'

Two weeks aboard the 'General Wayne'
is little more than a floating hospital
    vomiting spells. I attribute them to
      is truly ill. For two days he has
      in his bunk.
        Belle seems to recover. At least
         fretful which indicates improvement.
        struck by a nervous disorder.
I sleep very little and take no solid food.
                 (*page torn*)

(*Second page*)
Yesterday evening poor little Cookie died.
She was seized suddenly with spasms, poor thing,
and died in an hour. You will accuse me of
                        but it was truly frightful.
                        I have not slept for weeping.
                        only a dog!
                                                (*page torn*)
(*Third page*)
            arrived safely in New Orleans but
                embark. We are all in quarantine
                    might be better, but Belle is
                        all day by her bedside. Doctor
                            plague and gives me no hope
                                pray for survival.
                                                (*page torn*)
(*Fourth page*)
            have not been able to put pen to
                        all over. Our dear little girl
                        among the blessed, my beautiful
                            authorities let no one near.
                            darkies. I am full of
            one who was without fault and so
                        lies shrouded in my sister's
                            blame God and myself, dear
                    why you have left me without support?
                                                (*page torn*)

A blunder rectified: A final word from Cincinnati businessman, Reuben Chandler, to his runaway wife

Nor do I wish to prolong this tired debate.
I will be brief therefore.
I arrived back from New York late
to find your letter.
So be it.
It was never in the book of my mind
to hold you by force
if I could not restrain you
by the bonds of wifely affection.
Consider yourself free.
On one condition.
That you send both boys to me
entrusting, by law,
their future to my direction.

Of the causes of strife between us—
your selfishness, your vanity, your whims, wife,
your insistent and querulous disobedience,
no more.
It is enough for you to live with your naked conscience
upon which must lie the death of our infant daughter
as her innocent body lies, unfulfilled, in its grave.
Farewell.
Find peace if you can with your sister,
her friends and fashions.
Frivolity is an armor of lace
against the mind's inner vengeance and poisons.

I shall send the boys abroad for their education
as soon as I am advised of a suitable school.
Respect my will with regard to the bills of divorce.
Direct all correspondence to my lawyer, Mr Duval
(you have his address).
Now amen to this farce.

R.C.

A successful American advises his sons studying abroad:
Reuben Chandler to his sons in Geneva

NOVEMBER 5, 1859   **CINCINNATI, OHIO**

My dear sons,

I have just received Monsieur R's term report
and am much pleased.
He says you work diligently and faithfully.
Such work, my sons, prepares you for the time
when you will be men in this our own rich country
where labor is the standard of nobility,
idleness, wretchedness,
and careless indolence, a sin
against the Creator whom we worship.
For here we are judged and respected
according to the work we accomplish.

Summer has passed away
and the beautiful fall,
and now we have winter with its

bitter snows and winds.
Yet, on careful inspection do we find
that nothing is evil or ugly in God's Universe,
but all is for His good and wise purpose.

When you were young
you put to me many questions which,
when I could not answer,
made you cry.
Now you are wiser and older
and know as I
that religion to the mind
is as nourishing food to the body.
Little need, therefore, to urge
or admonish you.
Read your Bible with attention
and the Great Book of Nature with understanding
and you will find in both revealed
Our Good Deity,
His World in all its glory.
His just laws under which we live.

Business is good.
We number one hundred fifteen persons, store and
        factory.
All have more to do than they can accomplish.
It will be a busy, pleasant place when you return . . .
to follow with humble spirits and pure hearts
the peaceful ways of commerce and just economy.
Nanna sends her love. Dear little Lottie

begs you come and admire her frocks and pets.
She is a bright spirit, and if we live,
will be a source of joy to us continually.
And now, my dear boys, trusting you to continue well
and to work honorably, I remain your affectionate father,

R.C.

Letter to a mother from a Confederate soldier:
Matthew Chandler (aged 18) to Marianne Lavalle
Chandler, divorced by Reuben Chandler in 1855
Directed to an address in New Orleans

FEBRUARY, 1864   **A CAMP IN TENNESSEE**

Beloved Mother,

You have left me too long, all alone,
in the land of the despot.
God grant that I soon may be able to set us free.
From this day forward I hate every Yank, as my father.
From him I scorn to take quarter, as
to him I refuse my surrender.

I arrived in Tennessee, quite safe, without any
    hindrance,
though I shook in a fever of vengeance all the way.
I begin this day in earnest my work of murder.
With God's help I'll shed a whole river of

Union blood. Then Hell be my portion
if I don't make my sweaty horse swim in it!

Yours from your loving son,

Matthew Chandler

NOTE: *Matthew died of wounds in a Washington hospital in 1865.
Marianne died, the rumor is of drink, in New Orleans in 1872.*

Notes to a father from a young man gone West: Jacob Chandler to his father Reuben Chandler

NOTE: *These few pages were written, presumably to his father, by
the young Jacob M. Chandler in 1867. Although much of this let-
ter has been lost, there is reason to believe it was written as a sort of
journal on a voluntary expedition to Colorado, and was posted in
excerpts en route whenever possible. Jacob M. Chandler spent two
years in the West gaining experience as a surveyor, a miner and a
sheep rancher before he returned (poorer than when he set out) to
take over the family clothing business in Cincinnati.*

SUMMER, 1867   **COLORADO**

So we struck across the mountains, travelling for two days
without sight of a human being. At dusk on the second
evening, we drew rein on the summit of one of those lofty
hills which form the spurs of the Rocky Mountains. The
solitude was awful. As far as the eye could see stretched an
unbroken succession of peaks, bare of forest—a wilder-
ness of rocks with stunted trees at their base, and deep
ravines where no streams were running.

A gleam of light at the bottom of the gorge caught our Indian's eye. Descending the declivity we reached a cabin rudely built of dead wood brought down, probably, by spring rains from the hills. We knocked at the door. It was opened by a woman holding a child of about six months. She was scrawny and lined, I would have guessed fifty, but she said later she was thirty. She gazed at us searchingly for several minutes, and then asked us in and provided us with milk and corn-bread, a welcome meal.

The cabin was divided into two apartments, a kitchen which served also as store-room, dining room and sitting room; the other chamber was the bunk room where the family slept. Five children of all sizes tumbled out of this latter apartment and stood gawking at us from the rough-adzed doorway while we ate.

The woman said her husband was a miner. Four years before he had come with the family from the East. Pushing on in advance of the main movement of immigrants in the territory, he had discovered a rich gold placer in this gorge. While he spent his days working it, his wife, with her own hands, turned up the soil in the nearby valley, raised all the corn and potatoes required for support of the family and made all the clothes.

We asked if she had ever been attacked by Indians. 'Only twice,' she replied. 'Once three prowlers came to the door and asked for food. My husband handed them a loaf from the window, but they lurked in the bushes all night. Another time a large war-party encamped a mile below us. A dozen surrounded the house. We thought we were lost. We could hear their bullets rattle against the rafters, and you can see the holes they made in the door. We should have all been scalped if a company of soldiers had not come up the valley that day and burned the redskins out.

'There is no end of bears and wolves. We hear them howling all night. Last winter the wolves came and drummed on the door with their paws and whined piteously, like big dogs begging for their dinners. My husband shot ten and I six of them. After that we were troubled no more.'

When we asked her if she were not lonely, she gave a little cry, whether in laughter or anguish I could not tell. 'I'm too busy to think,' she exclaimed, 'in the daytime. I must wash and boil and bake and look after the cows who wander off in search of pasture. I must hoe the corn and potatoes and cut wood. We have no schools here, as you can see, but I have taught the oldest children how to read. Every Sunday we have family prayers. We each read a verse of the Bible (except the baby) and then the children repeat it until they know it by heart.'

We finished our meal and thanked her and gave pennies to the children, who took them without looking at us and then scuttled off into the pitch darkness of the bedroom. She said she would have liked to ask us to pass the night there, but she and her husband were hard pressed to find beds for their own brood. 'One day,' she confided to us, 'we shall have a fine house with two storeys and a carpet and some proper English china and I shall want for nothing. We are saving for a saw mill, and by next spring should have our own lumber business and maybe a drayhorse or two.'

After we had watered and rubbed down our horses we said good-bye. For a long time after we left I saw her standing by her unpainted door every time I looked back.

She stood in the sun, frowning as though it dazzled her. I could not help hoping she would at last have her fine house and her saw mill. As we were obliged to reach Denver by the next day to pick up a mining party, we pressed on through most of the night. We camped, finally, in the shelter of a boulder, and I went to sleep praying for that strange, brave couple who had chosen to risk their lives for the sake of a little gold, a saw mill and perhaps a set of proper English china.

Maxims of a Christian businessman: From the journal of Jacob M. Chandler, Cincinnati's citizen of the year 1895

The Foundations of Belief

1. Christ demands full surrender
2. Give Sunday to the Lord
3. Alcohol is Satan's most powerful weapon
4. No man is beyond redemption

A Guide to American Home and Business Ethics

Work is next to Godliness; a man should keep books when dealing with the Deity.

The Golden Rule of the New Testament is the Golden Rule of Business.

Religion is the only investment that pays dividends in the life everlasting.

By doing good with his money a man, as it were, stamps the Image of God upon it and makes it pass current for the merchandise of heaven.

Advertising makes Business articulate. It is a language of faith between buyer and seller.

'Labor is life! 'Tis the still water faileth.
Idleness ever despaireth, bewaileth.
Keep the watch wound or the dark rust assaileth.'

Have faith. Only believe that you can lick a man and you can lick him!

No day seems long enough to those who love work.

We have no one to fear except ourselves.

To have no aim in life is next door to committing a crime.

Let a boy's first duty be to his conscience, his second to his home because there is a mother there, his third to the welfare of his country.

Everything can be determined by the three little words, 'Is it right?'

Money has feet and walks away, but right habits are abiding.

Economy, like charity, begins at home.

The path of virtue leads through the valley of sacrifice.

Body and soul must go hand in hand to reach the goal.

Smiles are roses along the way.

A worried father writes to his daughter at Oberlin
College: Jacob Milton Chandler to his daughter Maura

MAY 5, 1896   **CINCINNATI, OHIO**

Though not altogether unsuitable, my daughter—your
letters abounding in girlish merriment—allow me to
suggest that accounts of such frivolous and literary pas-
times as you and your fellow scholars (or should I say
scholaresses?) choose to indulge could be significantly
improved by some small attentions to spelling and the
principles of grammar. A sterner critic, or one less fond,
might find in your latest scribble (you correctly term it)
intimations of carelessness unbecoming in a woman
of grace and intuitive decorum.

Yet, my dear, I am willing to concede that a person
of your temperament, torn from the bosom of her loving
family, must (if she does not weep out her days in melan-
choly remembrances) stride into the rough world more
than a little giddy with the ebullience of youth and the
lighthearted gaiety of irresponsibility.

I do not reproach you for your laudable, if unfeminine,
desire for a share of the world's knowledge. My advice is
to delight while you may in the manifest abundance of
God's world, provided that while you rejoice in this life
you remain sensible, always, of that which is to come.

I am distressed, however (and make no attempt to
dissemble my feelings), that you chose and deliberately
chose to pass so few hours with your brothers, your
mother and myself this past Easter. Your excuses (your
studies, your scribblings, your acquaintances) make few
amends for your sudden and inexplicable withdrawal from

the family circle. Rather they augment the pain you have caused us.

Did I speak for myself alone, I could not in conscience complain. A father must provide for his own. Your debt to me is not one deserving of acknowledgement. That I have worked, yea toiled, for your health and wellbeing full seventeen years of your life has been an unbegrudged sacrifice. Yet once, in his days of poverty and misfortune (days you will not remember, you were but a babe), your father vowed never to darken the familial hearth or diminish by a shade the brightness of your mother's eyes through the slightest reference to his burdens in private business. This vow he has kept! To this day, as you know, no shadow from the world has darkened the glow of my household.

Yet your mother suffers! Suffers, I believe, through the thoughtlessness of that being who should now be her greatest comfort. For it is you, my child, who have occasioned the loss of her beauty, health and good cheer which, throughout your childhood, so encouraged and nourished your own. Next time you are at home, Maura, notice her careworn face. Her hands once whiter than yours. Her fine strong shoulders, stooped with the years of childbearing. Think, my daughter, of who it was by your bedside when, swollen with fever, you lay in your tainted sheets, poisoning the air with your breath. Who was it who comforted you, embraced you, was at all times ready to cure, with the magic of a kiss, the bruised knee or cut finger of the plaintive child who ran weeping to her?

Maura! Maura! Those kisses were never gifts! Bestowed as they were with the charity of Our Lord Himself, those kisses were loans! Loans upon interest these many long years! Now it is time to repay them, graciously, selflessly, with little acts of kindness and understanding. For think, my dear, if you were ill, how that face would appear like an angel's hovering above you, its every wrinkle a wavelet of sunshine. Hers. Who will leave us one of these days! Yes, burdens, increased by your burdens, unless lifted, will break her down. Those hands that have done so much for you will lie crossed on a lifeless breast, and those lips, those neglected lips, will be closed forever.

This admonition I send in the spirit of Love. Its purpose is not to rebuke but to touch, to remind you of duties which ambition, it may be, has obscured. With it I send my blessing, in the hope . . . nay, in the belief and knowledge that you will return to us a New Woman. Gentle. High hearted. Self-forgetful, with a sweet and winning interest in all the little things of the home, to shed upon us all and upon your mother in particular, the divine luster of Christian Peace which alone can illuminate and make radiant forever
The Kingdom of Home.

From your loving and affectionate Father,
J.M. Chandler

A New Year's message to myself: From the journal
of Maura Chandler on the eve of her marriage
to Ethan Amos Boyd

JANUARY 1, 1900   **MOSSY HOUSE,**
                                       CLEARFIELD, VERMONT

Without false pride.
Without true faith.
With little hope
and with no glad energy,
but still, thank God,
steeled firm in belief
that there is a right way
and a wrong
through our human loneliness,
I begin this New Year's
Day of my life in marriage.

Cold. Midnight-morning.
Candlelight out in the cold.
Oval on the near side
and the far of the
mimicking window.
My face on the far side
and the near. My life.
This room that I know,
doubled also, hung
there in the snow.

So the unknown begins as
reflections of the known.

Perhaps it was never meant
that I work as I intended.
Perhaps it was never meant
that I write, learn, elevate
myself as I intended.
My vocation. My mission.
What does Nature
ask of Woman?
Give to him that needeth.
Employ the hour that passeth.
Be resolute in submission.
Love thy husband.
Bear children.

For now it behoves me to
crush out all personal sorrow,
forsake the whole ground of
self interest, ask not,
'Do I love him?' but affirm!
'It is good! It is right!'

If I keep every moral commandment,
fulfil every physical requirement,
feed mind into heart,
proffer heart to humanity—
stands it not then to reason
a woman will be happy
in her season?

I do not believe it. How
can I believe it

when the darkness comes?
When there, out
there in the snow
hangs a mockery, room
through which those huge,
slow ghost-flakes amble and fall!
Failure and suffering,
tedium, childbearing,
disease, deaths, days—
burying us all!

Yet without false pride,
without true faith,
with little hope
and with no glad energy,
I am, dear God, firm,
firm in belief
that there is a right way
and a wrong
through our human wilderness.

I begin, in this room,
this year of my life and marriage.
I begin, in this room,
this New Year. My life in marriage.

A vigorous letter from a salesman of the Lord:
Ethan Amos Boyd to his wife Maura

Blessed One,

I think of you hundreds of miles away, and of our dear
green innocent Vermont and reconcile myself with diffi-
culty to these torrid streets. If it were not for Faith, for
my earnest Belief that Spirit is All and the ALL THINGS
REAL proceed from it, I think I should find Business un-
bearable. My love, I am alone among the Sadducees!

It is to preserve my ideals in this Egypt that I've taken
to playing Moses and have drawn up a set of Tablets
which, my dearest wife, I am eager to share with you that
you may be better instructed in my simple ways.

Eschew	*Engage in*
Late Hours	Early Bed
	(Never After 9.00 p.m.)
Stuffy Rooms	Daily Exercise
White Bread	Brown Bread
Animal Food	Raw Vegetables
(Flesh and Fowl)	
Alcohol	An Occasional Pipe
	(for me)
Gossip	Philosophy
Novels	Mercy
Expense	Baths

I am pleased to say I have been successful in keeping
to this regime, and feel the better for having eaten noth-
ing but vegetable food this past week.

I have had time to make one or two public addresses; on Sunday to the Ethical-Social League and yesterday to the Women's Trade Union Association. The Unions face a shortage of money which your father, among others, could do much to remedy were he Christian and high-minded as he pretends. He is not *positively averse* to our turning Mossy House into a workers' retreat, but only skeptical as to our making a profit from it. I tell him that is not of account!

Whatever his opinion, I shall rise up from this city with my flock within a month. If he distrusts my means, tell him purposes like mine have for centuries fed the hungry and clothed the naked. Yea, even as a Salesman of the Lord shall I succeed.

I exist, my angel, in the invisible radiance of your trust. When I ponder on your loveliness, on the woman-liness of females and on the sleeping allegory within that veils their Sphinx-like secret, I marvel that Man has deserved propagation in this wicked world.

Until we meet I survive on your letters,
Your devoted husband,
Ethan Boyd

THE CLEARFIELD ENQUIRER

JUNE 2, 1929

The State of Vermont, County of Clearfield in Insolvency

Notice is hereby given that the Honorable Wm. A. Shapley, Judge of the Court of Insolvency and for the said county of Clearfield has issued a warrant against the estate of ETHAN AMOS BOYD of Mossy House, Clearfield Town in the Said County, an insolvent debtor; and the payments of any debts and the delivery of any property belonging to the said insolvent debtor to him and for his use, and the transfer of any property by him, are forbidden by law.

A meeting of his creditors will be held at the Court of Insolvency in Burlington on the 10th day of June next, at 9.00 o'clock in the prenoon, for the proof of debts and the choice of an assignee or assigness.

Horace Coleman, June 2, 1929
Deputy Sheriff

*A Letter to God on hotel notepaper
from Ethan Amos Boyd*

NOVEMBER 3, 1929   **HOTEL RIVIERA,
TROY, NEW YORK**

Dear Lord,
I am ill, I know,
from my own earnestness.
I am stumbling-foolish.

Everything I have wished to do, to be . . .
No. I have not done. Not been.

I have no learning or acquaintance
with learned colleges or degrees.
I have no profession or any patter
the world calls manly or
gentlemanly. I have no money.
Except as I sell Thy word
I am rot in my family . . . mine,
my daughter's center.
My home—happier without me.
My wife—silent.
For long periods, completely silent.

One baby we lost.
He was one or thereabouts.
His mother even yesterday,
after twenty years, in tears for him.
And now this turbulent, gifted,
unfinished nearlygrown son.
Unnecessarily,
the doctors agree.
(Curious, Lord, that both should be
taken unnecessarily.)
Fifty. Fifty-three.
And only these fumbling hands
with which to continue fighting.
This sick mind and bad eyesight
quivering between Thy Love and my fear.
To keep one from the strength of the other.

PART TWO

Women in Marriage
1930–1968

*A London letter: The poet, Kay Boyd, replies
ambiguously to her sister in Clearfield*

NOVEMBER 11, 1968   **HAMPSTEAD, LONDON**

Your letter arrived with its letters
   lunging at my conscience.

     Alone in wet London

with the wind trailing rain
   around these ugly brick villas,
      and the four o'clock night

arriving with my late lunch,
   I ask myself often
      why it is impossible to go home?

Why is it impossible,
   even here,
      to be peaceful and ordinary?

The ordinary offers itself up,
   can be eaten, breathed in.
      It counts on being dependable.

This is a window.
   This is an apple.
     This is a girl.

And there is a cyclamen—
   blood climbing out of the ground.
     And there is a blind of rain.

And now between the girl
   and the flower-flame on the window sill
     the window is a blur of rainwater.

I wonder how she felt, Persephone,
   when she bit for ever into the half-moon
     pomegranate?
     Did she miss ordinary things?

She could have lived
   without risking the real fruit.
     There were only six seeds.

She willed to eat nothing else.
   It was hunger.
     Without nourishment how could she live?

Eating, she lived on through
   winter after winter,
     the long year perfected,

the cold, waking rain
   raising a few seeds to green
     from her creative darkness.

But the mother smiled and smiled.
　　She was brilliantly consumed, a sacrifice
　　sufficient for each summer.

Should any daughter blame her?
　　The mother made her choice.
　　She said her 'no' smiling.

She burned the kissed letters.
　　She spat out the aching seeds.
　　She chose to live in the light.

Would you wake her again from the ground
　　where at last she sleeps
　　plentifully?

*Two Cambridges: A letter from Maura Chandler Boyd
to her daughter Ruth Arbeiter in England*

JULY 2, 1930　　　　　**CAMBRIDGE, MASSACHUSETTS**

Dear Ruth,
　　With the wedding six weeks behind,
　　and the whole country, so it seems,

tilted sideways and ready to
　　slide right off the world
　　like a plate of oysters,

there you are in the one Cambridge,
   and here I am
      in the other.

As father used to say,
   'The true life of the intellect
      secretes an impregnable cocoon.'

Guess what? I've bought you an ice box.
   Also a huge bed, big enough for four.
      At a charity sale for the unemployed.

Everybody says I'm crazy,
   but suppose you two come back
      without a job or a house or

a bean to buy a beefsteak?
   Everything you own these days
      is an investment.

Now for your wonderful letter!
   To think of your getting to Cambridge
      in time for that ball!

What did they give you to eat?
   Was the food fresh? They tell me
      the English don't know how to cook vegetables.

I'm grateful for the snap of King's Chapel.
    It brought tears to my eyes.
        To think how poor father would have loved it!

I meant to warn you, Ruth,
    before you left. I've heard the English
        take a light view of drink.

Greta's nephew, Fred,
    came back thoroughly *amazed*!
        He said he saw Christian women in public saloons!

But then Greta says that Fred
    came back with all sorts of notions.
        He said—since you're our poet—

there's a young man from Harvard—
    you ought to know about him. Eliott?
        Something like Lawrence Eliott.

I don't suppose it matters.
    These new-fangled writers don't go deep.
        Not like my beloved Dickens.

Now I must catch a train and hustle up to Clearfield
    before Philip and Sue, who are
        driving there all that way!

Give my best love to Neil
    and tell him to keep an eye on you.
        Who, dear, is Bloomsbury?

Don't be too impressed by those aristocrats.
  Hold up that pretty head
    and be proud you're a free American!

                    As ever,
                        your loving Mother,
                            M.B.

*A letter from an English novelist: Paul Maxwell,
author of 'A Second Eve', writes to Ruth
Arbeiter in Vermont*

21 OCTOBER, 1936   SOUTH KENSINGTON, LONDON

Two years ago. Only two years, and the terrible chasm
between that autumn afternoon in a Vermont pasture
and that unknown spring or autumn morning when we
will meet again grows wider and wider. So you have two
daughters now! Kathy and Eden. Eden and Kathy. Two
American girls.

    The impact of your letter was such that I almost see
you. You and your baby in that big shabby kitchen with
the broken floorboards hidden under the patchwork rug,
and the clay mugs marching along the high shelf over the
hearth. There. I *can* see you clearly. You are holding the
baby in the crook of your left arm while with your right
you are pouring water from a jug into a large stoneware
basin set solidly on the scrubbed table. The water is just
the right temperature. You question it with an elbow to
make sure. Gently, you are laying the poor naked scrap in
the womb-like basin.

She howls immediately, but you are serious and firm. You rouse the soap to lather and you wash the head (the black mane you describe). Then you carefully wash limbs and belly, taking care not wet the navel which is not yet healed after its brutal severing from the placenta.

The baby is perfectly clean and perfectly frantic. You remove her, redfaced and howling, to a salvational towel. Tenderly (but again, seriously, thoroughly) you dry the thicket of hair, miraculous hands and feet, the little runnels and pleats of the fleshier thighs. Vigorously you powder each inch. You snow sweet powder into the delicate rift of the buttocks. Finally, you pin on the nappy (you, of course, call it a diaper) and slip a fresh muslin nightdress—gently, so gently—over the baby's head, taking care not to damage the life-giving palpitation of the fontanelle.

When you sit down it is in one of those plain unpainted rocking-chairs, polished by generations of your grandmothers. You unbutton your blouse. Not Leonardo, not Raphael, not Bellini has on canvas depicted such dazzling, inflammatory white breasts. But you, of course, are unaware of their beauty. For you, they are not lilies, nor succulent apples of honey; nor are they two 'breasts dim and mysterious, with the glamorous kindness of twilight between them'. No. They are practical technical instruments for nourishing your child. The greedy thing pummels and sucks. The milk flows too swiftly. The child splutters, chokes, has to be balanced over your shoulder for a painful winding.

But now at last she has settled into a rhythm of felicitous satisfaction. She is happier, perhaps than she ever will be again in her life.

You? Are you opening a book? Yes. You take a book everywhere even now. (You keep a book, still, in your handbag when you wait for a bus or go to the dentist.) So you open what is lying on the table . . . is it *The Rainbow*? Is it my collection of War Poets?

The baby has stopped sucking. It is asleep. You hardly notice. Ruth, you are not reading at all. Instead you are staring out of the window where a simple frill of muslin frames (I remember precisely) a harvest of red and orange hollyhocks.

Dearest, I am dreary in London where everyone bores me with German politics. I'm so vehement in my campaign to get back to the States, my friends have ceased drinking with me. I bore them to distraction with encomia.

Nourish me with a long letter. *Eve* progresses slowly (tell me if what I have written here about your baby seems suitable for the novel). I return two poems of yours, unfortunately rejected, but redolent as always of

my own dear Ruth,
your Paul

Two Poems and a Rejection Slip:
From the notebooks of Ruth B. Arbeiter
1936

VERMONT AUTUMN

We have come to the end of a summer in this gold
season.
The year trembles.
I stare down these vistas of light, emblazoned with leaves,
as into the future of the past—its silence and memory.
The empires are asleep there.
Egypt and Europe.
They are locked in each other's stone arms
legible as geology.

Oh, pharaohs and princes buried in the dust of dead
legends!
Are you resentful of Time that has stripped you of
meaning?
Did you, like these leaves, burn away in gold rust into
rest?
Or did you, like trees, only counterfeit
wanings and deaths?

Can you feel in old roots the new energy coiled in this
continent?
Can you fructify as it reels out in wave after wave after
wave of imperious shimmering?
Look!
It surrounds you with a halo, now golden,
now pulsing and green!

THE SHORT AND THE LONG DAYS

All in the spell of the short days
We passed as it were through a mine or maze
Which was Time's interminably coiled cave.
No help nor any hope he gave,
Nor miracle of answered prayer;
Nor would he for our asking send
The slightest pin-point candle there
To light our end.

Groping along the hours, we clung
To them like ledges. Minutes hung
From our necks in leaden spheres
As, pendulum-like, they counted days as years.
Then change of sun made Time our friend.
Look how he lights with sky our ways!
How short the distance to the end
Of these long days.

THE POETRY REVIEW

The Editor regrets that he is
unable to make use of your
MSS. He is grateful for the
opportunity of considering
your work, and is sorry that
pressure of time makes it
impossible for him to write a
personal letter.

A Love Letter:
Ruth Arbeiter to Major Paul Maxwell

SEPTEMBER 3, 1945   **CLEARFIELD, VERMONT**

Dearest,

You must know that I think of you continually,
often entering unexpectedly
that brighter isolate planet where we two live.
Which resembles this earth—its air,
grass, houses, beds, laundry, things to eat—
except that it is articulate,
the accessory, understanding, speaking of
where we are born and love and
move together continually.

Departures are dreams of home,
returns to bodies and minds we're in the habit of.
And what are these terrible things
they are taking for granted? Air and grass,
houses and beds, laundry and things to eat—
so little clarity, so little space between them;
a crowd of distractions to be
bought and done and arranged for,
drugs for the surely incurable pain of
living misunderstood among many who love you.

One evening not long ago
I walked to the high flat stone where,
as children, we used to lie in wait

for the constellations. It was dusk and hazy,
the hills, soft layers of differentiated shadow
thick with the scraping of crickets, or katydids,
or whatever you call those shrill unquenchable insects,
sawing their way through night after summer night.
Seated on the stone,
straining into the distance,
it was strangely as if I were
seeing through sound. As if an intensity,
a nagging around me, somehow became the mist—
the hills, too, breathing quietly, the sun
quietly falling, disappearing through gauze.

Such seeings have occurred frequently
since we were together. Your quality of perceiving,
a way through, perhaps, or out of, this
damaging anguish. As when we looked down—
you remember that day—into the grassy horse pool
where one bull frog and one crimson maple leaf
quietly brought our hands together.

Dearest, what more can I say?
Here, among my chores and my children.
Mine and my husband's children. So many friends.
And in between, these incredible perspectives,
openings entirely ours in the eddying numbness
where, as you know, I am waiting for you
continually.

Ruth

From an Asylum:
Kathy Chattle to her mother, Ruth Arbeiter

MAY 2, 1954   THE GOOD SAMARITAN
                                HOSPITAL, NEW YORK

Mother,

If I am *where* I am
because I am *what* I am
will you forgive me?

God knows I have fought you long enough . . .
soft puppet on the knuckles of your conscience, or
dangling puritanical doll made of duty and habit
and terror and self-revulsion.
At what cost
keeping balance on invisible threads?
At what price
dancing in a sweater set and pearls
on the stage sets of your expectations?

Yes she was a nice girl!
Yes she was good!
Got married. Had a baby.
Just as she should.

Her head was made of walnut
His body of wood.
Then they had a little baby
made of flesh and blood.

Oh mother, poor mother!
Daddy thinks I'm wicked.
Here they think I'm crazy.
Please think I'm dead.

Dead, yes, and watching
from that safe, safe distance.
There. Your stubborn shoulders.
Tight smile
Head in relief, tilted a little,
tense with controlling intelligence.
How can I make you believe
I am myself—a self—
only when dying alive?

Without some interior self-murder
I am blank, void.
The face which I know must be watching
but is never there.
To the flow, you might say, of my experience
what a screen is to the flow of a film.

When I had little Libby, yes,
I was almost real.
But used. Used up.
Almost killed, being able to feel.
'Motherhood will settle her nerves,'
Daddy said, who was never a mother.
I knew in the coil of my head
how I hated her! Hated her!

Christ, how she howled!
And nothing I could feed her . . .
my milk, canned milk, powdered milk, goat's milk . . .
nothing would soothe her.
The doctor? Sympathetic but busy
And I, pouring breastmilk and blood . . .
uncontainable tears . . .
Once, in a quiet hour, I wrote to you.
Frank burned the letter.

He had begun to be gnawed.
Fine unseen teeth were
gnawing him . . . whittling him.
Wife
forcing him into the prison of a family,
Baby
shaping him into the
middle class, money-earning
ulcered American Dad
Frank's maleness, idealism . . .
self-flattering, easy conceit
never could admit.

Remember when he bought us that
crazy red, ramshackle farmhouse?
Miles out in the used-to-be country?
Well, his sports car, his sideburns,
his scotch tweeds and 2 a.m. barbecues
gave our wife-swapping, beef-eating neighbors
some unthreatening entertainments!

But by that time we were enemies.
By day hardly speaking.
At night, mutual and experienced torturers.
Libby, our principal weapon,
spun helplessly between us.

'Don't take your venom out on the child!'
Frank would yell at me.
Then whisk her out in his MG
To the zoo. To the park.
One day he brought her back
bloodied by a swing.
It was late. Dark.
I didn't say anything.
Called the doctor. Made bandages.
Filled up on whisky.
Later on, both drunk,
he threw me down the cellar stairs
'Slut!' he kept shouting.
'Slovenly, drunken bitch!'
Which was close to the truth.
I never could live with my life
unless I was drunk.
I never could sleep or cry
until I was drunk.
I drank all day.

One week Frank went away . . .
just one of his conferences . . .
and Libby came down with 'flu. A fever.
But she wasn't that sick.

Just sick enough to slash nerves into strips.
Moaning and vomiting
whining and bullying . . .
Panic like a hornet in my brain.
Even my diet of whisky couldn't keep me sane.
No. Don't you tell me she's only a baby.
You know as well as I do, dear,
that babies have selfish grown
bitch personalities curled up in them . . .
like molars or hair.
When she screamed
she knew she made me scream.
And when I screamed,
she knew I screamed guilt.
Mother! Can't you feel what I felt?
I had to get out of there.
For her sake. For her sake. I . . .
Mother, I wished she would die.

So I slept myself sober.
Installed my crone baby-sitter.
Drove to the station.
Took the first train.

It was one of those days when
April is like October. Rain
through a wind full of
knife-edged, excitable sunlight.

Walking from Central Station
feeling slenderer, blonder . . .

familiar shiver of pleasure when
men stopped to stare.
Sky again! Younger.
Too scared to go to bars . . .
wandering like a schoolgirl from
museum to museum . . .

The Modern Art. The Guggenheim.
The Frick. The Metropolitan.
At the end, in the end
to the Cloisters.
You took me there often as a child,
you remember? Your small puzzled
prudish fat daughter!

But weirdly, mother, weirdly,
this time it was just as before.
Just as hallowed and hushed and mysterious.
Just as drenched in its greyness and gentleness.
As if I'd been waiting there somewhere . . .
some part of me waiting in childhood,
expecting myself to come back.

There was one chapel . . .
could I have dreamed it?
Crouched, resigned, half-caryatids,
shouldering the arches like sins . . .
on the altar, stiff, under a baldachin,
a statue, a crude wooden Mary
dangling her homunculus son.

She was worn, wormeaten,
hunched in the vestiges of drapery.
Her features? Weary.
Weary and purposeless with suffering.
Her face? Void. A wound of
perpetual suffering.

And she stared at me, down at me,
suffering, out of one
glazed terrible eye.
I took in that gaze like a blade!
What was it? A threat or a lie?
Or did she know?
Her thin Christ had no head!
But did she know?
I don't know what I did,
or why. It blurs now, but I
woke up to find myself here
where they've taken my belt and my
wedding ring, where they
specialise in keeping me weeping.

Come when you can, or when
the whitecoats let you.
But they may not let you, of course.
They think you're to blame.
Good God, mother, I'm not insane!
How can I get out of here?
Can't you get me out of here?

I'll try, I'll try, really,
I'll try again. The marriage.
The baby. The house. The whole damn bore!

Because for me, what the hell else is there?
Mother, what more? What more?

Mrs Lillian Culick, divorcée, to Dr Frank Chattle

MAY 21, 1954   **THE CENTER FOR RESEARCH IN
URBANIZED HUMAN BEHAVIOR,
DEPARTMENT OF SOCIAL PSYCHOLOGY,
BLYTHNESS COLLEGE, NEW YORK**

Darling,
Or may I still Frank?
Or should I kneel?
'Sir.' 'Dr Chattle'
so . . . salutations from your patient
patient. Anyway, be
decent, dear, and don't destroy me
yet, although you're livid,
I just know it,
at the lie of this
departmental envelope.
But I've tried to write, to
phone so often, Frank, each
empty, echoing evening.
Even if we're through
it's unmanly not to
meet me, not to discuss
us, not to confess.

Does this purposeful burying of
reasons mean you're
banking on a bust-up Frank?
Won't you take a share
of the blame? Well,
I don't know what game
you were playing, but I swear
Kathy's hangups were never
sparked off by *me*!

Ruth phoned and jabbered on
hours about your kid.
She can't know anything.
She'd forget I was
Pollyanna Sunshine
if she walked in and
found us in bed!
                    Oh,
let's skip the shit
honey!
I've been in a mood.

Be nice.
I need you.
To be with.
To talk to.
My depression's come back
and I'm living on Valium.
I can't eat.
I can't talk.
I don't know what I want.

Could it be the cut we've
made in our sex life?
I've got some queer shakes.
I can't chew. I
can't sleep. I'm always so
dizzy with Seconal.

Can't you guess what I want?

Well, it may not be you,
Frank. Yes, damn it, I'm
not sure you'd do
in the long run. Oh, you
talk too much and you
kid around too much. You
let yourself down. You know
I never wanted us to be
lovers in the first place!

But I think you understand me.
Won't you make me happy?
Remember what you wrote
about my bones?
I love your little poem
about my bones and my
muscles like dolphins,
and the sea life in the
tides of my skin.

I'll not whet your appetite because
I *don't* know what I want.

So don't come.
Not tonight, anyhow.
Perhaps I'll drop in
at your office tomorrow.
I could do with a
prescription.

I'm all nerves
and I can't swallow.
I've lost five
pounds out of guilt!
(I wish there were some
safe pills for guilt.)

Oh Frank.
Have you felt what
I've felt?
Will you forgive me?
For this letter?
For this agony?
Don't be angry.
I've been lonely.
Let's try to meet soon.
                    OK?

End of a summer's day:
From the journal of Ruth Arbeiter

JUNE, 1968   **THE STATE HOSPITAL, BENNINGTON**

Dreaming or dying? The room as usual.
Ceiling and woodwork, whites of a calm grey eye.
Curtains in motion. Membranes between myself and the
screaming of the locust. Bed-cage. Locker.
Aluminum pitcher and tray. Neil in the guest chair,
his bought flowers like blood spots.
Why carnations in rose season? Habit.
No, kindness. No, habit of kindness.
An artificial smell all the same.

As when I was waiting for father in that hot
hellish hospital in Cambridge after Jimmy died.
Jimmy. Would be now fifty . . . nine. At twenty
a comedian. Grotesque, all nose and glasses, fuzz for
      hair.
Poor mother's two-hundred-brush-stroke Sundays . . .
still it would never lie down. 'Ruthie,' he whispered,
'run back and fetch me my specs, there's a sister,
and a morning paper.' That between the night's
      operation
and at noon being dead. Mother at her best brave,
      praying.
Phil gone for Dad. I, bulky, alone, eighteen,
in the aseptic corridor, hating that I was hungry.
'I am selfish,' I thought, crying about that.
'I can't be unhappy enough.'

College days. Ohio in the nineteen-twenties.
It might just as well have been the nineteenth century.
Our philosophy reconciling Christ and Darwin.
Our Modern Lit embarrassed by Wilde. In those
      days . . .
those sandwich days before the Crash I hardly noticed,
before Belgium and Pearl Harbor and Auschwitz—
senseless un-American disasters which destroyed, but
never touched me. Left me a litter of conveniences.
My life. Our double life, poor Neil's and mine,
in Boston, in Cambridge . . . Harvard's
      Cambridge . . .
so many brilliant, miserable, significant people.

They would have frightened you, Dad, who followed,
stumbling, in the footsteps of your Maker . . .
His footprints too deep for you. Your hurt face peering
      over.
Dear Dad, dear failure, dear
specialist in injured feelings!
Did you guess how we lived on our tip toes,
towards the end of it, Mother and I?
Every purchase a crisis. Every meal a negotiation.
While you waded away in the swamp of your
      complaints,
telling everyone that everyone was against you until
everyone *was* against you, and they took you away,
blind, sick and mad, a disquieting absence at my
      wedding.

Amazing. It is amazing.
Your face. Very clear.
Can you see me? Can you hear me?
I know that, like me, you intended to live a long time.
You admired old age and its accumulation of
    understanding.
You looked forward to seeing me, half mother,
half Virgin, surrounded by the halo of your
    grandchildren.
Borne aloft, perhaps, by hundreds of little children!

There. That locust again.
Insect anguish stretched past the limits of restraint.
Jet scream through the blue above the lake.
June and July.
The Children in the rock pits, bristling with tin spades.
They called it 'The Fortress' that crevice in the boulder
where Kathy—in her red striped jersey—and Eden—
    always
skinny, bony, shivering—played and played.

The wind up suddenly.
                'Time to pack up now.'
                    'Oooooh!'
a wail in chorus. 'Please, Mommy, one last swim,
    Mommy!'
'One. Then we go.'
Nicholas, his sunburned body curled hot on my thigh,
is asleep still, in his blind skin.
But the girls splash in carelessly as frogs.
The waves flutter.

The little moored boats, each doubled by the lake,
loosen their masts across the querulous water.

Of course, this is the loss that you prepared me to
prepare for, Paul. That June and July.
Waking beside you at no hour . . . leaning for love
     over
rare wine gone sour in the glasses . . . ashtrays spilling
     over
into books we were never able to get to the end of . . .
nights we were never able to get to the end of . . .
love into sleep and sleep into love again,
telling time by a laughable hunger or the
slow spreading path of the sun in the dust, on the
     wallpaper.
Dearest Paul. Suppose we had gone back . . . or on.
Would it have been different?
Would you have changed us all?

The question ceases to matter before the question is
     resolved.

I think I must have thought too often of your thoughts.
Whether of me, or, more likely of your new book . . .
unfinished. Like your life, unfinished.
Never begun, really, never committed to anything so
self-defining as a name, a place, a family . . . anything
that might twist the eddying possibilities
into a frame around you. Not a failure, like Father.
Not a liar like myself . . . who finds, not you, but this
usual earth strange to take leave of.

PART THREE
Living for Now

Professor Arbeiter to his dead wife

AUGUST, 1968   **CLEARFIELD, VERMONT**

The worst time is waking
                    as if every nerve were working
scalpels in the running wound, knives in the gash.
For in life, love, nothing begins or ends with a clean
        crash.
The brain knows, but habit is like cash or clothes.
It continues its momentum like a blind weight through
        glass.

I can't lie down in the dark with your severed voice,
        Ruth.
In this room full of trivial attentions I am still your
        guest.
'You're cold, dear. Let me fetch you your rug.'
'You're tired, I know. I'll tell them you need to rest.'
Here. Again. On the phone. Overheard in the hall,
'I'm sorry. My husband is working. At seven? I'll tell him
        you called.'

Ruth, in our thirty-six years lost to eye-strain and bad
     temper
you never spoke to me once of what I know.
I neither dared nor dared not to speak to you, though
sometimes your inattentions drove black words like
     swarming insects
swimming in held-back tears through my desperate
     paragraphs.

I was proud of you, Ruth. My girl.
My critic. My helpmate. Hostess to a pack of fools
you could always smile at. Confidante of students
too shy to seek me out. Friend of all milkmen and maids.
One day. One June, you gave tea to Isaiah Berlin.
And invited our Clearfield carpenter.

These last years have been . . . what, Ruth?

Living with someone who's dying. Not letting her know.
And she, although not told, knowing.
As though the courtesy of our mutual lie
were drawing us together under its canopy.
I read to you. Henry Adams. You had so much to say.
You asked for a handkerchief the last day. Impatiently.
          As if death were a head cold.

I dream most nights of a garden. Formal. Like
     Versailles.
Laid out in terraces, box hedges, sculptured old
gods and goddesses.
                    We are walking together on a gravel path

when suddenly the vista changes. Frames of ash
are descending in geometrical patterns
                            to a dry fountain.

But the worst is waking.
Reaching for the radio through the strings of your voice.
Listening to the whining of hillbillies, over and over.
            Closing my eyes
        as if the night could never be over.

Nick Arbeiter writes poems on the road
to Wyoming after a funeral in Vermont

JULY–AUGUST, 1968

            I
(*Albany*)
West, man, West.
            I'm being fed to my own bogged veins!
Know yourself. Your inheritance.
Self-hating. Self-abasing.
            How we eat of ourselves!
'Just the family,' father said.
                            Death was real.

Then the crows flocked in
                    trained for crises,
to deck out a flesh corpse like waxwork,
to croak hoarse Amens to a long box,
to peck out old photographs.

Christ thought he could sell us the straight gate
                    if we paid him in sacrifice,
if we gave up the apple of knowledge
                    for his extraordinary wine.

But Christ's Presbyterian blood for her was grapejuice.
His narrow gates opened to the total wind.

I remember they made her smile
for the earth seeping in
                    through the aisles of her abandoned body,
        eroding it,   book and pew.

        II

(*Akron*)

Waking up every morning in a different city
which is always the same city in a different place
with always the same woman sprawled adrift in the
        sheets
as if lost in the confusing surfaces of her names . . .

how soft it feels floating up through the old gauze
        places.
Hollyhocks and blue wallpaper,   stones,   resonances,
        window-glass watery as a lake.

Two little girls and a woman reflected among the bright
        leaves.
They shimmer there inverted in a glaze crimson as
        sumac.
They are beautiful,   they smile at me,   they invite me
        to drown.

Now an air conditioner bores me with monotonous
     stories.
A window, flowered with curtains, frames me a Greek
     façade.
That strip of red neon must have been left on all night.
It flashes mechanically   VACANCIES   VACANCIES.

My last night's girl shrouds her breasts,   moans for
     coffee.
Doors slam in the dew-drenched cars.
                                   Their engines start up.

III

(*Scotts Bluff*)
In Nebraska it's the moon.
Mario's Steakhouse and Bar in the middle of the moon.
Ramshackle leftover, left over U.S. 20.   102 Fahrenheit.
                         Clay   wind   and sand.
The dry waves in rings around the wrecks of meteorites.
Slabs of eroded igneous. Tongues out at the stars.

Tonight there is empty thunder over the white bandage
     of the highway.
Occasional cars are missiles,   are implorers . . .
voices wailing to rain gods locked in the dry horizons.
Walking in crimson dusk or in scalding wind.
Wading through the sediment of ages cleft for no
     one . . .
these are the world's negations. This is the wilderness.

Scotts Bluff. Bleaching like a relic in the North Platte's
wandering incision in the dead sheet of the Plains.
Pleistocene valleys rucked up in raw clay, claws
reaching to root out and tear up all inhabitants and
      habitations.
Jaws, incisors unappeased by city names . . .
Jail Rock and *Smokestack Roundhouse* and *Twin Sisters*.
They will not be made flesh. They will not accept
      parables.

At one time, in the ice age, there would have been a
      glacier here.
Bedded in alluvium the teeth of Tithanotherium.
Bones of Merycoidodon,   Poebrotherium in fleshy clay.

The dry creeks are shot thick with millennial flints,
with the dust of the dog-sized horses of the dust of
      Pawnees.

IV

They say to you
    whatever is in your mind.
       The white sands.

V

(*Laramie*)

At every motel the formica boys
       swagger in with their chromium girlfriends.
The restaurant rocks as the juke box slings out
      hits from a two-years-stale menu.

I smoke in a corner booth, take in the floor show.
The girls with their leathery eyelashes and fringed
      thighs.
The boys with their low-slung belts, their sharpened
      shoes.

'Let it be, let it be' and rock-a-bye-baby, Daddy.
You taught us discretion in a woman
          was worth all the dollars in Hollywood.
No one could have bought you equipment to play your
      own wife.

We knew her moods like the roads in our New England
      county.
You knew her like a map
          you could depend on to get to your
             destination.

VI

Palms up cupping the globe of his twelve-year-old
      cognac,
Father reminisced and accused himself.
Neighbors called on tiptoe, bearing jam and casseroles.
Bald Maxwell quoted Keats and got drunk.

'When I think of the waste, the sheer waste,' Father
      maundered.
'And with so much to give and to live for . . . '

'She gave us her light,' agreed Maxwell.
'She burned out her love for more of us than she could
      afford to.'

VII

It's dangerous to live in a noose of 'I want' and 'I ought'.
Antaeus, held too high by Hercules, broke his root to
    the soil.
Our race thins. We're second growths
             fighting for what's left of the sky.

VII

We accuse you, fathers,
            we accuse you of lies.
of pouring out a smoke screen
          of high-minded fervor,
and then setting off to murder
        under twin banners, Profit and Compromise.
We accuse you of signing on
         with Corporation Hypocrisy,
of willing us a money machine
        that feeds us by consuming us like fuel,
of letting cities rule
      while the grass withers and the
rivers pullulate with acids,
        of setting up houses like music boxes where
love is only wound up once
      and then allowed to run down.
We accuse you of using reason
        to sanction massacre,
of making freedom
        a one way street with barbed wire.
We accuse you of not understanding
        even now why you are what you are,

though under the asphalt
        there rises a burning savage
and over his ashes
        you glide in a soft mirage.
Will you have time to hear us
        who go easy and barefoot?
who are earthbound in airports?
        who are flesh among cars?
Will you give us your deserts
        and let us bring life there?
Will you watch us making love
        between your carports and skyscrapers?

We are weak.
        We are human.
            We are unsure.
We train our few possessions
        to stand under us like ankles.
We like dreams.
        We like trips.
            We've got a Hell you've never been to.
Black or white,
        men are miracles to us.
Sick or poor,
        truth is sustenance to us.
Waking or dreaming
        they're the same thing to us.
So that there be peace among the animals.

Epilogue: Kay Boyd to her father, Professor Arbeiter

JULY 4, 1972   **HAVERSTOCK HILL, LONDON, N.W. 3.**

Dearest Father,

This is the anniversary of our loss.
I write to the shushing of trees outside my window
(London planes, sycamores in Massachusetts)
Watching them sift light restlessly on a tiny garden.
The leaves are palm-shaped, like New England maples,
but the wind drags them aside like a loose drapery
as if trying to expose some savage or gipsy origin.

Our maples never stooped to be voluptuous.
They were prim New England. Trim domes. Upright
    clouds.

Yes, leaves sweep away from the trunks of these English
    trees
the way mist lifts from her farms.
The bark is like topographical shading
Or the shadings of accent and stone in this wrinkled
    country.

'Come back,' Eden wrote, after mother died.
'Come help me to keep her alive a little longer.'

But I didn't go back because I couldn't see what to come
    back to.
I couldn't think who to go back as.

That Kathy my name was, that Mrs Frank Chattle
died in New York of divorce.
Kay Boyd, the woman, the writer, has survived.
She lives a long way from Eden. The tug back
is allegiance to innocence which is not there.

'In the floodtides of *Civitas Mundi*
New England is dissolving like a green chemical.
Old England bleeds out to meet it in mid-ocean.
       Nowhere is safe.'

It is a poem I can't continue.
It is America I can't contain.

Dear Father, I love but can't know you.
       I've given you all that I can.
       Can these pages make amends for what was not said?
       Do justice to the living, to the dead?

BIOGRAPHICAL NOTE

INDEX OF TITLES
& FIRST LINES

BIOGRAPHICAL NOTE

Anne Stevenson was born in Cambridge, England, in 1933, the eldest daughter of the American philosopher Charles L. Stevenson and his wife, Louise Destler Stevenson, both from Cincinnati. She grew up in New England and Michigan and studied music, European literature, and history at the University of Michigan, where she received her B.A. in 1954 and her M.A. in English literature in 1961; she was a winner of a Major Hopwood Award for poetry in 1954. Her first major poetry collection, *Reversals*, was published by Wesleyan University Press in 1965. From the 1970s to the late 1990s, she published many volumes with Oxford University Press, including *Correspondences* (1974), *The Fiction-Makers* (1985), and *Four and a Half Dancing Men* (1993). Her four volumes of poetry with Bloodaxe Books (Northumberland, England) include *Poems 1955– 2005*. She is the author of *Bitter Fame* (1989), a biography of Sylvia Plath, and of two studies of Elizabeth Bishop, most recently, *Five Looks at Elizabeth Bishop* (1998; Bloodaxe, 2006). She settled in Britain in 1964, where she has lived in Cambridge, Scotland, Oxford, the Welsh Borders, and more recently in North Wales and Durham. She received the inaugural

Northern Rock Foundation Writer's Award in 2002, and in 2007 the Neglected Masters Award from the Poetry Foundation, the Aiken-Taylor Poet of the Year Award from the *Sewanee Review*, and a Lifetime Achievement Award from the Lannan Foundation.

INDEX OF TITLES
AND FIRST LINES

A backward May, with all the local finches, 91
A day opens, a day closes, 92
A house with a six-foot rosewood piano, 85
A memory kissed my mind, 49
A mother, who read and thought and poured herself into me, 73
'A wind blows through the clock,' 100
After a long drive west into Wales, 77
After the Fall, 34
After weeks of October drench, 55
Aged by rains, 20
Ah Babel, 26
Angel, An, 77
Ann Arbor, 5
Another day in March. Late, 24
Arioso Dolente, 73
As I Lay Sleeping, 70

Beach Kites, 99
Before Eden, 92
Between, 20
Black Hole, 53
Bloody Bloody, 51
By the Boat House, Oxford, 17

Casual, almost unnoticeable, 13
Circle, The, 21
Cold, 47
Coming Back to Cambridge, 13

Consider the adhesiveness of things, 97
Contending against a restless shower-head, 87
Correspondences, 103

Dr Animus, whose philosophy is a table, 25
Dream of Stones, A, 43
Dreaming of the Dead, 38
Driving south from Hereford one day in March, 96

Elegy, 65
Enigma, The, 95
Enough of Green, 19
Enough of green, 19

Falling to sleep last night in a deep crevasse, 95
Fiction Makers, The, 39
Fish Are All Sick, The, 31
For mapmakers' reasons, the transcontinental air routes, 33

Garden of the Intellect, The, 4
Generations, 12
Granny Scarecrow, 79

Habits the hands have, reaching for this and that, 80
Haunted, 84
Hearing with My Fingers, 85
Himalayan Balsam, 29
How in this mindless whirl of time and space, 90

I believe, but what is belief? 38
I dreamed a summer's labour, 43
I have grown small, 53
'I think I'm going to have it,' 10
I went down to the railway, 36
If I Could Paint Essences, 24
In the house of childhood, 63
In the Tunnel of Summers, 32
In the Weather of Deciduous Souls, 90
Inheriting My Grandmother's Nightmare, 97
Is this a new way of being born? 99
It is imagination's white face remembers, 21
It's not when you walk through my sleep, 84

It's too big to begin with, 4
I've lost a sense. Why should I care? 81

Journal Entry: Impromptu in C Minor, 55

Know this mother by her three smiles, 12

Lady, / I've not had a moment's love, 34
Landscape without regrets whose weakest junipers, 7
Leaving, 80
Letter to Sylvia Plath, 59
Like threading a needle by computer, 76
Living in America, 3
'Living in America,' 3
Lost, 54

Making Poetry, 42
Marriage, A, 86
Meniscus, 22
Mind led body, 72
Minister, The, 18
Moonrise, 75
Mother, The, 11
Moving from day into day, 32

Neither city nor town, its location, 5
North Sea off Carnoustie, 15
Not my final face, a map of how to get there, 88
Now I am dead, 83

Of course I love them, they are my children, 11
On Going Deaf, 81
Orchid-lipped, loose-jointed, purplish, indolent flowers, 29
Orcop, 96
Other House, The, 63
Out of the afterlife behind my eyelids, 70

Path, 20
Poem for a Daughter, 10
Politesse, 49
Postscriptum, 83
Price, The, 23

Ragwort, 17
Red Rock Fault, 35
Report from the Border, A, 84

Salter's Gate, 45
Saying the World, 71
Sierra Nevada, 7
Siskin, 12
Skills, 76
Small bird with green plumage, 12
Small Philosophical Poem, 25
Snow. No roofs this morning, alps, 47
Sole to sole with your reflection, 44
Somewhere nowhere in Utah, a boy by the roadside, 5
Spirit Is Too Blunt an Instrument, The, 9
Spring comes little, a little. All April it rains, 27
Still Life in Utah, 5
Stone Milk, 91
Stone-age, stone-grey eyes, 54
Sun Appears in November, The, 22
Surprise on the First Day of School, A, 72
Swifts, 27

Tears flowed at the chapel funeral, 79
The beasts in Eden, 69
The fear of loneliness, the wish, 23
The fish are all sick, the great whales dead, 31
The moon at its two extremes, 22
The spirit is too blunt an instrument, 9
The way you say the world is what you get, 71
The wet and weight of this half-born English winter, 20
The worm in the spine, 82
There, in that lost, 45
They are great healers, English springs, 59
They belong here in their own quenched country, 17
They give you a desk with a lid, mother, 72
They won't let railways alone, these ragged flowers, 17
This hot summer wind, 68
This is the South-West wind, 35
Time to go to school, cried, 48
To Phoebe, 90

To witness pain is a different form of pain, 82
Trinity at Low Tide, 44

Variations on a Line by Peter Redgrove, 100
Vertigo, 72

Wars in peacetime don't behave like wars, 84
Washing My Hair, 87
Washing the Clocks, 48
Waving to Elizabeth, 33
We were the wrecked elect, 39
We're going to need the minister, 18
When my mother knew why her treatment wasn't working, 86
When the camel is dust it goes through the needle's eye, 68
When trees are bare, 22
Whenever my father was left with nothing to do—, 65
Where the Animals Go, 69
While my anxiety stood phoning you last evening, 75
Who I am? You tell me, 51
Who's Joking with the Photographer? 88
Why don't you Vermonters call October, 90
Willow Song, 36

'You have to inhabit poetry, 42
You know it by the northern look of the shore, 15
your tower allures me—, 26

AMERICAN POETS PROJECT

1. EDNA ST. VINCENT MILLAY / J. D. McClatchy, editor

2. POETS OF WORLD WAR II / Harvey Shapiro, editor

3. KARL SHAPIRO / John Updike, editor

4. WALT WHITMAN / Harold Bloom, editor

5. EDGAR ALLAN POE / Richard Wilbur, editor

6. YVOR WINTERS / Thom Gunn, editor

7. AMERICAN WITS / John Hollander, editor

8. KENNETH FEARING / Robert Polito, editor

9. MURIEL RUKEYSER / Adrienne Rich, editor

10. JOHN GREENLEAF WHITTIER / Brenda Wineapple, editor

11. JOHN BERRYMAN / Kevin Young, editor

12. AMY LOWELL / Honor Moore, editor

13. WILLIAM CARLOS WILLIAMS / Robert Pinsky, editor

14. POETS OF THE CIVIL WAR / J. D. McClatchy, editor

15. THEODORE ROETHKE / Edward Hirsch, editor

16. EMMA LAZARUS / John Hollander, editor

17. SAMUEL MENASHE / Christopher Ricks, editor

18. EDITH WHARTON / Louis Auchincloss, editor

19. GWENDOLYN BROOKS / Elizabeth Alexander, editor

20. A. R. AMMONS / David Lehman, editor

21. COLE PORTER / Robert Kimball, editor

22. LOUIS ZUKOFSKY / Charles Bernstein, editor

23. CARL SANDBURG / Paul Berman, editor

24. KENNETH KOCH / Ron Padgett, editor

25. AMERICAN SONNETS / David Bromwich, editor

26. ANNE STEVENSON / Andrew Motion, editor